UNDERCOVER OPERATIONS SURVIVAL IN NARCOTICS INVESTIGATIONS

ABOUT THE AUTHOR

Tony Alvarez has been a police officer for twenty-one years with the Los Angeles Police Department. The last sixteen of these years he has been assigned to work in the field of narcotics enforcement. He is presently a Detective Supervisor in charge of a narcotics detail.

In the last eight years he has conducted classes and seminars which deal with undercover operations and officer survival and he presents training in local agencies throughout the nation. He has instructed at the F.B.I. Academy in Quantico, Virginia, the U.S. Customs in Los Angeles and San Diego, and is a lecturer for the California Narcotics Association at their annual conference and local training sessions.

UNDERCOVER OPERATIONS SURVIVAL IN NARCOTICS INVESTIGATIONS

By

TONY ALVAREZ

CHARLES C THOMAS • PUBLISHER

Springfield • Illinois • U.S.A.

Published and Distributed Throughout the World by

CHARLES C THOMAS • PUBLISHER

2600 South First Street

Springfield, Illinois 62794-9265

© *1993 by* CHARLES C THOMAS • PUBLISHER

ISBN 0-398-05871-7

Library of Congress Catalog Card Number: 93-13542

With THOMAS BOOKS *careful attention is given to all details of manufacturing
and design. It is the Publisher's desire to present books that are satisfactory as to their
physical qualities and artistic possibilities and appropriate for their particular use.*
THOMAS BOOKS *will be true to those laws of quality that assure a good name
and good will.*

Printed in the United States of America
SC-R-3

Library of Congress Cataloging-in-Publication Data

Alvarez, Tony.
    Undercover operations survival in narcotics investigations / by
Tony Alvarez.
        p.   cm.
    Includes index.
    ISBN 0-398-05871-7
    1. Undercover operations—United States.   2. Drug traffic—United
States—Investigation.   I. Title.   II. Title: Undercover operations
survival.
    HV8080.U5A44   1993
    363.4'5'0973—dc20   93-13542
                                                                CIP

PREFACE

Undercover work is some of the most dangerous and complicated type of investigations which can be undertaken by law enforcement officers. No one in this field has all of the answers with which these officers can operate and conduct those investigations. Most of the expertise developed in the field of narcotics enforcement is a result of on-the-job training. More experienced officers train the younger officers.

In this book I have attempted to relate my experiences and the experiences of officers with much expertise in this area. Even after spending seventeen years as a narcotics investigator, I find myself learning new ways in which to operate and conduct undercover operations. I have travelled extensively throughout this nation. I have been fortunate enough to instruct agents from the FBI, the U.S. Customs Service and numerous local law enforcement agencies. I have found that narcotics officers are yearning for knowledge in this area. Their questions display the fact that their training is minimal at best.

This book was written, as a reference, to be used for years to come by officers involved in the field of undercover operations. The stories which I cover are real cases. These have been painful occurrences which caused the deaths of some of the officers involved. I cover these cases in the hopes of giving the reader a better understanding of the principles which are outlined. Perhaps these cases would have been handled differently by other officers. It is my hope that the reader will be able to avoid committing the same type of mistakes if they were to undertake similar operations.

It is not my objective to criticize any of the agencies or officers involved in these investigations. These officers were and are heroes. Their mistake was costly and we should never undermine their decisions. Going over these cases, I attempted to point out those factors which I felt caused the breakdown in the operations.

While I do not single out, by name, any of the officers I have worked with, I must tell you that I am in their debt forever. Their dedication and professionalism are without par. I have been lucky to have been associated with many outstanding officers throughout my career.

I have met and worked with undercover officers who are the cream of the crop. They have taken their time in teaching me the tricks of the trade. I have personally made many mistakes while working in an undercover capacity. I have been lucky, avoiding injury, while working in an undercover capacity. Sometimes it is better to be lucky than smart, especially if it keeps one alive. However, we can not count on luck all of the time. I'd rather rely on expertise, experience and professionalism.

After working in law enforcement for twenty-one years it is difficult to dedicate this book to a certain individual or individuals. I think of the first captain or lieutenant who gave me a chance to work a section within narcotics, the partners who took me under their wing and taught me everything they knew and more, my family who put up with the long hours and the mood changes, the supervisor who believed in me and got me started in the field of undercover operations, those who worked for me and gave me their all, the district attorneys from the major violators section who prosecuted the good and the not-so-good cases I brought them, the California Narcotic Officers' Association who have presented outstanding training for all narcotics officers, and last but not least, all of my brother officers in other local, federal and state agencies who assisted me in cases and investigations which we worked together. All these people and others, whom I haven't mentioned, should be given credit. Without all of them, I would not have been successful in my quest to excel in the area of officer survival and undercover operations.

This book will keep the memory of our fallen comrades alive. Individuals like Blackie Sawyer, Norm Eckles, Tommy De La Rosa, Raymond Hicks, Kelly Key and hundreds of others whom I do not mention. These fine, dedicated officers must not be forgotten.

T.A.

CONTENTS

UNDERCOVER OPERATIONS SURVIVAL IN NARCOTICS INVESTIGATIONS

Chapter 1

UNDERCOVER OPERATIONS

U ndercover operations are used as a tool by law enforcement officers in the handling of certain types of investigations. While the under-cover investigation is most prevalent in the field of vice and narcotics, this type of operation is also utilized by other sections within law enforcement. Because undercover operations are used daily by narcotics officers, most of the examples and cases which we will cover will involve narcotics investigators and investigations.

The techniques and procedures which will be outlined throughout this book could be easily adapted to any undercover operation.

There is a danger which is inherited in any law enforcement operation; however, undercover operations are one of the most dangerous and challenging types of investigations. It is because of this that we find ourselves in need of much tactical preparedness prior to the investigation and close, continuing assessment during the operation. Unlike other operations, the undercover operation is a very fluid type of investigation. By labeling an undercover operation as fluid, try to visualize the operation developing as it unfolds. Without much planning this type of operation can proceed very rapidly from a normal situation to an explosive conflict. In an undercover operation this change occurs without warning and at the least predicted moment.

Under the best of circumstances and with the best planning possible, it is difficult to regain control of the operation and the people involved once a suspect or suspects decides to take lethal action towards the undercover operator.

Because of all the unknowns and the possibilities of harm occurring to the undercover operator and his covering team, it is most important that we understand the wide range of investigations and the planning necessary to execute a safe undercover operation.

It is also very important to undertake every undercover operation with much care and concern. This type of operation must not fall into the category of complacency.

As law enforcement officers we have seen our peers approach vehicles and houses with very little care and with no anticipation for safety issues. This holds true due to the fact that officers become complacent as they repeat procedures while in the discharge of their daily duties.

All of the law enforcement officers involved in undercover operations must not let complacency become part of their vocabulary, as it pertains to law enforcement operations (in particular undercover operations). There is no such thing as just another undercover operation. The safety and well being of the officers involved, in undercover operations, becomes the most important aspect of that operation. It must be the goal of the supervisor and all of the officers involved to place their safety as the most important factor. There is no investigation, suspect or amount of narcotics/money worth the life of an undercover officer or any member of the covering team.

Because undercover officers are considered experts in their field and because there are many factors which have a bearing in the outcome of an undercover operation, it is very important to note that for the most part undercover operations fail, approximately, 70 percent of the time. The failure rate has no bearing in the ability or expertise of the undercover operator nor the information received by that officer. Many other factors come into play such as, informant involvement, location of operation, the suspect's feelings toward the undercover operator and any other factor having no bearing on the operation as it unfolds but which is viewed by the suspect as a negative factor.

It is because of all of the unknowns, as the operation unfolds, that we must not forget what is the mission of the undercover operator and the covering team. Simply put, they are there to seize contraband, obtain evidence and arrest the violator. Even when a meet or operations is concluded without an arrest or any seizure of contraband, if the officers involved are safe to go home that night the operation has to be labeled a success.

To point out how outside factors and pressures have a bearing on undercover operations, I will recall an operation involving one of my partners who was negotiating with a suspect to purchase 5 kilos of cocaine.

Every time that the undercover operator met with the suspect the conversation and negotiations would go without a problem. After the meet, the surveillance team would follow the suspect to his house where the suspect would go into his back yard and remove a pigeon from a cage.

The suspect would throw the pigeon up and watch it fly away. Three separate times, after meeting the undercover operator, the suspect would go through the same ritual. Each time he would call the undercover operator back and tell him that the time was not right and that they would get together again in the future to consummate the deal.

On the fourth time the suspect went back home and repeated the same procedure. This time however, he came out with the 5 kilos of cocaine. He was arrested. During the interview we ascertained that his witch doctor (the suspect was a Cuban national and was a strong believer in the Santeria religion) had told him to throw a pigeon up in the air prior to doing any dope deal. The witch doctor told him that if the pigeon flew to the left not to do the deal, but if the pigeon flew to the right to go through with the deal. Needless to say the first three times the pigeon flew to the left. The last time it went to the right and the suspect went to jail!

It is easy to understand why these operations don't have a higher rate of success. As it was pointed out before, there are too many outside factors and pressures which will have an impact in the outcome of the operation. These types of obstructions will take place regardless of the undercover operators' expertise, planning of the operation and investigative work done by all involved.

Nonetheless, undercover operations are one of the most challenging and unpredictable types of investigations in law enforcement today. If done properly and safely they will bear immediate gratification to all involved.

Chapter 2

MENTAL PREPAREDNESS

There are three types of investigations which are most prevalent in the area of vice and narcotics enforcement. We conduct surveillance type investigations, investigations which originate with information supplied by an informant or any other source of information or undercover investigations.

Although all investigations must be undertaken with the utmost safety, it is important that each type of investigation or operation be analyzed. This becomes necessary in order to point out the mental preparedness of those involved and the likelihood of disaster that could result due to the suspects' actions or the compromising of the investigation by the officers involved.

If officers become involved in a surveillance type operation there is a chance that the surveillance could be compromised, with the suspect becoming aware that he is being followed. This would become apparent to the surveilling units by the actions of the suspect as the surveillance unfolds. At that time the units would terminate the surveillance and discontinue following the suspect. This is done in order to try and salvage the investigation and to preclude the suspect from confirming the fact that he is being followed (keep in mind that the suspects involved in the narcotics trade are overly paranoid and continually drive in a counter-surveillance mode, attempting to detect any type of surveillance by law enforcement officers). The surveillance will be continued at a later date. This type of compromise is the simplest kind and for the most part will not cause harm to any of the individuals involved. Because narcotic traffickers are constantly looking, it is very likely that a suspect will become aware that he is being followed if a surveillance is undertaken for long periods of time. Either way, the outcome would be to back off from the surveillance, letting him cool off, returning at a later time to continue with the investigation.

As a result of an independent investigation (such as receiving information from an informant or any other source), and or a surveillance, it is possible that officers could obtain a search warrant for one or more locations under the control of a suspect. During the preparations for the service of the search warrant, the case agent, after obtaining as much information as possible, will prepare a game plan detailing the entry, layout (if possible), any information regarding the suspect and premises and any other information which will be helpful to the entry and containment teams serving the search warrant.

After the planning of the operation, the briefing takes place. The entry and containment teams suit up and prepare to confront any eventually that is likely to occur during the execution of the search warrant. Every team member wears a bullet proof vest and all of the gear necessary to effect a safe entry.

Because of the high degree of danger in this type of operation, every team member is prepared mentally for a lethal confrontation. As professional law enforcement officers we train, as units, in the art of entries into all different types of locations. We are also aware that in any search warrant service and ensuing entry into a suspects' dwelling, the entry team could be confronted with deadly force. Since the mental preparedness of those involved is at its peak during such incidents, the entry team is able to defend themselves, return fire if fired upon and lay down cover fire if necessary in order to extricate any member of the team who has been shot or injured.

The entry team will retreat from the house, removing their casualties and setting a perimeter around the suspects' residence. After a perimeter is set, SWAT is called in to deal with the barricaded suspect. Again, all of the actions taken are procedures that have been practiced by the entry team. The mental preparedness of the personnel involved would be at its peak and the entry team would be ready for any and all type of confrontation or disaster that they encounter.

This type of mental preparedness, during the service of a search warrant, is the norm rather than the exception.

Let's now look at the mental preparedness of an undercover operation.

The supervisor, case agent and undercover operator call for the briefing of all involved. The briefing goes down without a problem and everyone knows their assignment.

The team sets out to cover the undercover operator. The officer who monitors the wire (this would be the officer who listens to the transmitter being worn by the undercover operator and relays the information to other team members) will take a place in the area, close to the meet location. The officer who has the point (this is the officer who will visually overlook the area of the meet, keeping the undercover operator in his vision) will also move close in and set up.

It is now that the mental preparedness comes into play. If the team covering the undercover operator has been involved in numerous fruitless undercover operations, their guard will relax and it is at this time that the complacency factor comes into play. Most of the covering team is not able to be involved in the inner workings of the operation, other than to await some kind of direction from the supervisor or the monitoring/point officers.

The direction, that these other team members will receive, will range from arresting the suspect to following the suspect or suspects away from the meet location or aborting the mission for whatever reason.

It is sometimes very difficult for the team officers, who are covering the area, to maintain their alertness under such conditions.

Another factor, that is sometimes overlooked, is the fatigue factor. Due to the nature of the job, officers assigned to a vice/narcotics detail work long hours. Because of the hours involved in the investigations the fatigue factor should be considered when planning an undercover or any other type of operation.

As we cover mental alertness it is very important that all undercover officers and their covering teams realize that no one can stop a lethal attack on the undercover operator from taking place. This is a very important point, a point which must not be forgotten or overlooked. The covering officers and the undercover operator can only react to an attack from a suspect. If the undercover operator goes into the operation without mental preparedness, the confrontation may well result in the death or serious injury to that undercover operator.

Covering officers must realize that in an undercover operation we become reactive instead of proactive.

Envision an undercover operator who meets a suspect at a large parking lot. During the course of the negotiations the suspect, for whatever reason, decides to attack the undercover operator. For the first few moments of that attack, (in my experience that time is between 10 seconds and 1½ minutes; the response time by covering officers depends on many factors that cannot always be planned) the undercover operator is on his own. The undercover operator must survive the attack while attempting to buy precious time for the covering team to arrive at his location. This precious time becomes the survival time.

If that undercover operator has not made up his mind that he will do everything in his power to survive the attack, it will be very likely that the suspect will gain the upper hand and overtake the undercover operator. Again this will result in the death or a serious injury occurring to that officer.

As stated before, undercover operations are very fluid. It will take the suspect a few seconds to attack the undercover operator. At the offset of such attack, the closest officers to the scene will be the wire monitor and the point man. These officers have to have the experience to react swiftly and decisively. Again, other factors outside the control of those involved comes into play. The traffic in the area, pedestrian traffic, other possible suspects and access to the location where the meet is taking place. These factors will preclude help from arriving, in a timely fashion, to assist the undercover operator.

Mental preparedness, at this time, becomes an important part of the complete package. That includes proper game planning, motivation, the will to survive, being able to pick up the red flags as they go up during the operation and the ability to stay mentally alert and prepared through all of the ups and downs of the operation.

If we cover all of the procedures necessary in the planning and briefing stages, it will be likely that the operation will be safe and productive. I wrote this chapter prior to the game planning chapter because many officers believe that the planning and briefing of an undercover operation are just mere steps in attaining a successful operation. This is not true. Game planning and briefing are very thorough procedures which encompass the operation and the survival of those involved.

As a supervisor, I will not hesitate to stop an investigation if I feel that the involved personnel do not have the right frame of mind and mental toughness necessary to undertake the operation.

Much has been said about mental preparedness. That preparation means different things to different situations. There are many different types of ways in which an individual can utilize his mental preparation. For instance, an undercover officer must be prepared to defend himself if attacked, he must be able to make certain decisions without hesitation and without help from other members of his team and he must be able to handle any situations that arise. Any situations could develop into an explosive encounter and the undercover operator must be able to handle them with calm and total control.

As a young undercover operator, in the mid 70's, I found myself inside a suspects' house, negotiating with him to purchase 3 oz. of cocaine. The covering team was located outside the house. In this period of time, the unit that I worked for did not have access to a wire. I was on my own inside the residence and the covering team would wait for my signal in order to make an arrest.

While I negotiated with the suspect, the door bell rang. The suspect got up from the table and answered the door. I looked up to see an individual enter the residence. I immediately recognized the individual who had arrived as a suspect whom I had arrested the day before and was out on bail.

It was obvious from the demeanor of the arriving guest that he was quite under the influence of a narcotic. Both guys walked to the table where I was seated and the main suspect began to introduce the arriving suspect to me. I looked up, acknowledged him, continuing to negotiate with the owner of the coke.

While I and the owner of the coke continued the negotiations, the arriving suspect stared at me while stating, "You know, I know you from somewhere. I just can't place from where." This suspect continued saying the same thing over and over again. I became aware that sooner or later the guy would remember who I was. I turned to the suspect who owned the dope and told him that I was there to spend a lot of money and his friend was beginning to annoy me. The main suspect told his friend to cool it. The guy did everything but cool it.

I finally realized that this would be my chance to get out of the house. I would use the fact that the guest, who had arrived, had annoyed me. I wanted to leave before my cover was blown. I got up and told the suspect, I was negotiating with, that I was leaving. I asked him to call me back when he was ready to deal some dope.

The suspect looked at his friend and told him to leave, he was not about to lose the sale of cocaine to this guys' friendship. As the suspect began to leave the house he turned to me and said, "I know where I know you from!" I prepared myself for the worst. The main suspect jumped in and told his friend to shut up and leave, and that he was not interested where he knew me from. The guy looked at his friend who had just thrown him out of the house and exclaimed, "You'll be sorry."

With that he left the house and we completed the transaction. The covering team outside the house detained the first guy when he left.

They also arrested the suspect inside the house after the transaction was completed.

Both suspects sat at the station waiting to be booked. They made a pact to be more revealing to each other on future dealings.

I came close to having my cover blown and my safety jeopardized. I prepared myself and had practiced to handle any kind of confrontation, lethal or not, of this kind. Prior to going into an undercover assignment I would play the worse scenario that could happen in my mind. By doing this I became mentally prepared to face any eventuality that would arise while working in an undercover capacity.

Drug enforcement and undercover operations, in todays' climate, are more dangerous than in the 70's. This is true due to the following factors.

• Because of the harsh sentences in drug crimes there is an added incentive for the suspect to fight and flee.

• Many of the suspects involved in the drug trade are themselves users of crack cocaine and other mind-altering drugs.

• The fact that most of the suspects are foreign nationals and they have a different mentality towards law enforcement. They also have a propensity to use violence.

• The fact that the drug transactions involve large amount of currency.

• The fact that violence is a common part of the drug world.

All of these issues are of paramount importance in the way which officers plan undercover operations and should be part of the discussion during the planning and mental preparedness of any undercover operation.

Preparing for the Undercover Role and Investigation

Undercover officers/operators do not just appear one day and are blessed by someone into the undercover role. The art, and yes it is an art, of working in an undercover capacity is a talent that must be developed and cultivated.

I sometimes listen with amazement when officers talk about working undercover while stating that anybody can buy dope. While that could be a true statement on certain occasions, such as purchasing drugs in the street level, certainly not everybody has the ability nor the aspiration to become an undercover operator.

Another illusion entertained by some officers in the field of vice/narcotics enforcement is that the best undercover operators must be minority officers or female officers. I have personally found that great undercover operators come in all colors and both genders. As a matter of fact the only prerequisites that I find important for undercover operators is that they must be individuals and must be able to talk themselves out of any situation. With that in mind, one can then proceed to choose the right person for each independent operation.

After we have chosen the right officer for the operation, there are many other factors which will make the operation easier to complete. These are factors that are very elementary but are overlooked daily.

The undercover operator should think of the proper clothing to wear for the operation. If the operation is to be a one-time buy, for a $20 rock from a suspect standing on the corner, dressing is not a great concern. On the other hand, if the undercover operator is to meet a major narcotics trafficker and they are to discuss the transaction over drinks and dinner, then dressing becomes very important. If the undercover operator were to show to the meeting, with a major trafficker, wearing a 1970 polyester leisure suit, the operation would come tumbling down like a house of cards. Likewise, if the operator is meeting with a member of a motorcycle gang and his cover is the affiliation with the motorcycle gang lifestyle, then the dress and everything else in that operation becomes attached to that life style.

Again, depending on the type of operation, if the operation is long term or of high quantities of narcotics, the undercover officer should have some type of false identification on his person. If I had a dollar for every time a crook has asked me to show him my drivers license, I would be a wealthy man.

The undercover operator has to have access to a phone number, a number which he can give to the suspect (again this is if the operation will be an ongoing thing). This is necessary in case the suspect asks for a number where he can call the undercover operator. Of course, the operator can give the suspect a beeper or cellular number. Both are good tools to use. I will go one step further and will recommend an additional phone number to give out at this time.

The agency that the officer works for should have an undercover number that the officer has access to. That undercover number should be a number which has the capability to be forwarded. By forwarding the number to his home phone, the undercover operator can tell the suspect to call him late at night or at a certain time that the operator will be home. Of course the undercover operators' family would be aware that any incoming call could have been initiated by the suspect. It is important that the family members be made aware of the undercover name being used by the operator.

This type of phone access puts the suspect at ease. Imagine the undercover operator, whom the suspect is still trying to check out, trusting the man enough to give him his home phone number. When the suspect calls, the phone is answered by the operators' wife or kids verifying that the number belongs to the operators' residence. This would do two things for the suspect, right away he will believe that the undercover operator is not a cop and by so thinking, the undercover operators' job will become easier.

Being "put to sleep" is the term undercover operators utilize to describe a suspect who has bought the operators cover story and is at ease by the fact that the operator is all right to deal with.

It is very important for the undercover operator to have some knowledge of the dope or other contraband he is negotiating for. The suspect will be an expert on prices, how to test it, how the dope is packaged and how it is used. The undercover operator should have the same knowledge. If he doesn't, it will be very likely that he will not be able to carry on an extended conversation with the suspect regarding the transaction.

Again, depending on the amount of purchase that the undercover operator is going to make, it is very important that he has some kind of story ready in order to excuse himself from using any dope. One of the explanations which I have made in the past has been to say that after I buy the dope I will have to meet with my parole officer and he will want to test me in order to ascertain if I was using. Another excuse I utilized would be that I was buying the dope for a girlfriend who had a habit and that I would use the dope as an enticement for her to have sex with me. A medical condition could also be used. Whichever excuse the operator wants to utilize and feels comfortable with is permissible, as long as the operator goes into the operation prepared to use an excuse if confronted with the testing of dope by the suspect.

As a matter of course these types of excuses only become necessary when the operator is buying small quantities of narcotics. On the large purchases the use of the narcotics does not come into play.

Do keep one thing in mind though, if the undercover operator is going to use the excuse of being on parole he better have some knowledge about a prison, the prison that he was supposed to have done time in!

When the undercover operator begins his negotiations with a suspect regarding the purchase of large amounts of narcotics or other expensive contraband, it is important that he portray himself as the middle man working with someone else's money.

If the undercover operator is representing to be the owner of the money then he has no reason to talk to anyone regarding negotiations. By becoming a middle man the undercover operator can always break away from the negotiations under the premise of having to talk to the main man. This gives the operator an opportunity to go to a phone and talk to his supervisor or the case agent regarding the negotiations and to discuss any changes in these negotiations.

While an undercover operator is acting the part of a dope buyer, the important word to remember is acting. The undercover operator should not try to be something that he is not. For instance, if the operator has an expertise in old cars he should portray himself as a dope dealer with an expertise in old cars. This way the operator is credible. On the other hand if the operator was to portray himself as an expert in airplanes, not having an expertise in that area, the suspect could see through that in no time. More than likely the deal would fall apart. The undercover operator must be reminded that he is acting or playing the part of a dope dealer; he should not forget that he is a police officer.

There comes a part in any operations when the undercover operator must break away from playing the part of a dope dealer/buyer and that he must become an active law enforcement officer. The reason for stating this fact is because many undercover operators play their undercover role to the end. Sometimes this costs them their lives.

This becomes true when the undercover operator is attacked by the suspect whom they are trying to apprehend. Instead of advising the suspect of his identity he continues to maintain his undercover role. At the first sight of trouble the operator should identify himself as a law enforcement officer. The undercover operator must make sure that the suspect does not continue to believe that the operator is either an informant or another suspect. In the high stakes game of narcotics deals, criminals would not hesitate to kill an individual whom they thought to be an adversary or a police informant. Their killing a police officer would be a different story as many of the crooks would not harm a law enforcement officer.

The undercover operator has to be ready to talk to the suspect in order to calm him down. Remember that the undercover operator has to buy time in order to have his covering team roll in to help him with any deteriorating situation.

Last, but in my mind, one of the most important factors to consider by the undercover operator is weapon accessibility.

Personally, I will not allow any undercover operator who works for me to go into an undercover operation unarmed. It might seem incredulous that some undercover operators would operate unarmed but believe me, it happens all of the time. There are many reasons for the undercover operator to decide to go into an operation unarmed. Although these reasons will seem silly, you will hear excuses like, "My pants are too tight and I don't have a place to put the gun." "We made a deal to be unarmed." "The guy told me he was anti-gun so I don't want to get him mad at me." All of these excuses are very well taken by someone else; I believe that the undercover operator need be armed and that the weapon he is carrying should be in a location where he can get to it in case of need.

It does no one any good for the undercover operator to place a .25 caliber pistol between his legs wrapped by body tape or around his ankle in a holster (remember that most suspects carry their weapons in their waistband where it is easily accessible). If the need to use the weapon arose it would be impossible for the undercover operator to get to it if he is carrying it in an inaccessible location.

During most dope deals the undercover operator has to realize that the suspect will be armed and the fact that the operator is armed will not be a deterrent to the operation. As far as I'm concerned, the operator must carry a weapon which is accessible or he does not operate the case. There is no room for discussion on this point.

I met two outstanding narcotics officers who had been involved in a dope deal in Southern California. The two officers negotiated with the suspects to buy an amount of meth and to sell the suspects one kilo of cocaine. The agreement between the officers and the suspects was that none of the participants would be armed during the deal. Both suspects were newly released ex-cons.

The deal was to take place inside a hotel room and the first suspect showed up, alone, to check the premises. He was patted down by the undercover operators. The suspect checked the room to make sure that there were no guns present. One operator and the suspect left the room. The negotiations continued and a second suspect was introduced into the deal. This suspect was a large, muscular Samoan. Because of the negotiations and other factors the Samoan was never checked for weapons. By this time the two undercover operators had placed their guns inside the room. The guns were inside small male purses which were placed on top of a table by the front window. The undercover operator, who had left the room, returned to the room accompanied by two suspects.

With the two undercover operators and both suspects in the room, the deal came to its climax. It was at this time that the large Samoan pulled out a semi-automatic pistol from the back of his waistband and began shooting at the two undercover operators. The two undercover operators could not get to their weapons because they were standing about ten feet away from the table where they had placed them. In any event, they were doing everything in their power to get cover.

As luck would have it, the Samoan was not familiar with the operation of the weapon which he was utilizing and it misfired. The Samoan tried to repeatedly shoot both undercover operators but failed. The covering team, which was located in the room next door, was finally able to make entry into the undercover room and take both suspects into custody.

The deal was a rip off from the beginning and the plan was for the Samoan to kill both operators and take their money and dope.

I supervised a young undercover officer whose job was to buy narcotics from street dealers in the San Fernando Valley. On this day the officer had a female partner riding with him. The covering team was to cover them closely where ever they went.

The operators were instructed to drive into gang infested areas in order to purchase rock cocaine. Because of the obvious danger one operator always kept his service revolver under his right upper leg, where it was easily accessible. Both undercover operators drove into the dealing area and were approached by a gang member who asked them if they wanted any rock cocaine. As the gang member looked inside the undercover vehicle he saw the butt of the officers' gun which was exposed. The gang member backed away and stated, "Say homie, why you got a piece with you?" The undercover operator, without missing a beat, replied, "Man, I don't want to get ripped off, besides I got my old lady with me. Let me have a $20 rock."

The transaction was completed and the suspect was arrested by the

covering team without incident. While it was not the intent of the undercover operator to have his gun exposed so that it could be seen by the
street dealer, that fact did not deter the suspect from the dope deal and
the officer felt that by having the gun under his leg was the best way in
which to carry the weapon for accessibility.

Chapter 3

DIFFERENT RESPONSIBILITIES

Case Agent

The case agent is the originator of the case. Never is the undercover operator the case agent. The case agent will get the information from his source. For the most part, undercover investigations originate with an informant who is able to supply information or is able to introduce an undercover officer to a suspect or suspects involved in a criminal organization.

The case agent will do all of the background investigation necessary to identify the suspect or suspects involved, ascertaining whether they have a criminal background. He will also attempt to obtain as much information as possible regarding the method that the suspects utilize to deal their narcotics or other illegal activities, locations, if they have used weapons in the past, etc. Once all of the background work is done, the case agent will begin preparations for the first meeting to take place between the suspect, the informant and the operator.

Once the package is complete, the case agent will approach the undercover operator and explain the case to him, requesting that he operate the case. The case agent will give the operator the ability to back out of operating the case if he does not feel comfortable with it.

If the operator decides to operate the case, there is a chain of events that will take place preceding the first meet between the operator, informant and suspect.

The undercover operator and the informant have to get together in order for the operator to become aware of what has transpired between the suspect and the informant prior to the meet. There is no worse feeling, for an undercover operator, than showing up for a meet with a suspect and being confronted with some kind of information which was provided about the suspect by the informant—information that the operator was not aware of.

Once the informant and the operator meet and iron out their plan of

19

exchanging information on and about the suspect and each other, the investigation is ready to proceed to the next step.

The Supervisor

The next step is to present the investigation to the Supervising Officer. As a supervisor, having been both an undercover operator and case agent, I believe that it is very important to understand and control all of the egos involved in the operation.

Anyone involved in the field of undercover work will be able to verify that all the investigators involved in the field of undercover operations have large egos. The undercover operator wants the case to go because he feels that his undercover expertise and reputation are at stake. The case agent wants the case to go because the case is his creation and he feels that he must continually show his ability to complete cases in a successful manner.

The supervisor has to look at the investigation with many things in mind. First and of the utmost importance is the safety of all concerned. With that out of the way, the supervisor can continue in his quest to put together a team-type operation that will be successful within the constraints of the law, the policies of the agency and the policies of the section that he works for.

After discussing the operation and the background of the suspects, the supervisor sets the parameter by which the case will be operated.

The supervisor will tell the undercover operator and the case agent what he expects and makes changes, when necessary, in the operation.

The undercover operator will be told the boundaries of the case. The supervisor will tell the operator what he can and cannot do within those parameters. He is also told that if he steps outside the parameters, set by the supervisor, the case will be terminated without further notice. The parameters must be followed strictly by the undercover operator. A supervisor can not have an undercover operator making decisions and changing operational procedures as the operation develops. Keep in mind that the safety issue is the most important of all and it is impossible for the supervisor to continually adjust the operation not knowing what the undercover operator will do next. If the undercover operator is making changes as he sees fit, it is virtually impossible to cover him and guarantee his safety and the safety of all involved.

From the first time that an undercover operator becomes involved in undercover operations, he has to know that he can not alter the plan which is put into motion by the supervisor and the case agent. There are only two ways that the undercover operator can alter the plan, one would be with the concurrence of the supervisor and the other would be as a last resort, in a matter of life or death to the undercover operator.

The supervisor, the case agent and the undercover operator must have a plan ready in order for the undercover operator to escape to safety. This is necessary in the event that the operation and the safety of the undercover operator is compromised. For instance, if the undercover operator is taken hostage and there is no plan by which to correct the situation, it will be very likely that a disaster will occur. However, if the undercover operator, during the planning and briefing discussions, is told that at the first sight of a covering team member he is to fake a heart attack and fall down, he will be able to get out of the line of fire between the suspect and his covering team. This will clear the way for the covering team members to shoot at the suspect, if necessary, or take any other type of action to end the hostage situation.

The supervisor and the undercover operator will work out an array of signals, both visual and verbal, that will tell the officer monitoring the wire or the officer who holds the point, that the operator is either in trouble or sees something that necessitates the attention of someone in the covering team.

After the meeting between the supervisor, the case agent and the undercover operator takes place, the operation is ready to be placed into action.

It will be very helpful if the supervisor, in charge of an undercover operation, has extensive knowledge in the area of undercover work. This knowledge can be attained by having been an undercover operator and or a case agent of undercover operations.

The supervisor must be able to pick up on red flags which will be raised by the actions of the suspects and or the undercover operator during the transaction. If the supervisor in charge does not have the experience to pick up those red flags, he will not be able to stop a case which is headed for obvious disaster. It is likely that an inexperienced supervisor will not be able to detect a developing problem until it is too late. If the supervisor neglects to react in a timely manner or is unaware of a developing problem, the safety of the investigators involved will be jeopardized.

The bottom line is that the supervisor is responsible for the operation and the safety of those involved. Because of this, the supervisor can not let a seizure or an arrest dictate a change on the safety aspects of any operation.

The Undercover Officer

The undercover officer is an individual who has been designated by his supervisor to be the key by which we seize narcotics and other contraband.

His job is simply to gain the confidence of the suspects whom he is dealing with and to get them to do those things which have been planned and approved prior to the operation.

The operator must be flexible, mature, tacticly sound and able to follow directions. At times he will make decisions which will either save his life or the life of those who are in the area who are trying to protect him. He can not make changes as he sees fit, unless his life is in danger at that time (then all the rules are out the window) and he has to keep his supervisor abreast of everything that is taking place.

The operator will have as much, sometimes more, input into the operation as the supervisor and the case agent. If the operator asks for some type of change and that change does not violate a safety procedure, the case agent and supervisor should attempt to accommodate the request. Different individuals operate differently. The way in which an individual operates has to be suited to the personality of the individual operator.

Informant Debriefing

Let me relate to you two operations. The first one illustrates the need for debriefing the informant prior to meeting a suspect. The second illustrates how the supervisor sets the parameters by which the undercover operator will work.

As an undercover operator I was asked to be part of an operation involving the manufacturing of Meth. The suspect in the case was an individual from Berkeley, California—a love child with a degree in chemistry.

Because I did not at the time feel that it was necessary for me to meet with the informant, for debriefing, prior to the meet with the suspect, I went in cold and we met.

The informant made the introduction and excused himself leaving me alone with the flower child.

The suspect was a bright individual and began to talk to me, using chemical terms and an array of words that meant nothing to me. Sometime into the conversation the suspect came to the realization that I was lost. I, not wanting to look any more stupid than I already had been, told the suspect that I just wanted to take a look at the lab and proceed with the buying of the Meth.

The suspect looked at me and said, "Mike, (the informant), told me that you had a Ph.D. in chemistry." I was not prepared for the bomb which the suspect had just dropped on my lap. I was in a tight spot and had to figure out a way to extricate myself from the mess in which I found myself.

I looked back at the suspect and told him, "I think Mike must have been pulling your leg. I think what Mike told you that I was a Ph.D. and by that he meant that I was a pretty happy dude."

The hippie crook almost fell off of the chair laughing. He took me into his trust immediately. It was like we had known each other for years. He took me and showed me the lab and my team ended up arresting him.

The bottom line is that I was not prepared nor did I have any knowledge of anything that had transpired between the crook and the informant and by not having a debriefing with the informant prior to the meet I could have messed up the entire investigation.

This case turned out fine, but don't count on being lucky all the time. It is a lot easier to debrief the informant and go into the meet with as much knowledge as possible than to look stupid like I did.

The supervisor in this case did not ask nor did he demand that I and the case agent be briefed by the informant prior to the operation. Had the supervisor done that, the above incident could have been averted.

Parameters Set By Supervisor

The next case covers the parameters which the supervisor sets. I supervised a street buy team and there was a young female, undercover officer, who worked for me. During a night operation, I told all of the undercover officers not to take any suspects into their car and drive away with them for any reasons. The restriction was placed on them because we were not prepared to do a moving surveillance and a few days prior to the operation a dope user had been stabbed and robbed while transporting a dealer to a location to pick up some dope. The attack had occurred in the same area that we were working that night.

The team moved into the area, singled out for the blatant sales of rock cocaine. The young female officer was the first operator to drive into the location in an attempt to make a buy. I was the point man, I could not believe my eyes. I observed a suspect approach the undercover vehicle, he had a short conversation with the undercover operator and as he did so he entered the vehicle. The undercover vehicle, with the suspect and the undercover operator, pulled away from the curb.

Many things went through my mind. Was the officer being kidnapped? Is the suspect going to rob her? etc. As I started to tell the covering team to block the vehicle and take everyone into custody, the vehicle came to a stop and the suspect began to exit. I later realized what had happened. The suspect told the undercover operator that he would sell her the rock but that he would only do it if he could do the transaction inside the car. Once in the car he told her to drive and while she did so, the deal was consummated.

I had had very little time to make a decision. I would either have had to let the case continue, watching the officer drive away before making the arrest or I could have sent the covering team in to arrest everybody, including the operator. The arrest of the operator would be carried out in an effort to teach that young officer a lesson.

I opted for the lesson. I sent the covering and arrest teams in and stopped the case. By so doing, they were to arrest the suspect and the undercover operator. The arrest team was ordered to utilize a felony prone position, for both individuals, at the time of arrest. That undercover operator was placed on the ground (this was done in order to keep her cool), was hand cuffed and driven away.

When I met with her I was visually angry and explained all of the mistakes she made and the consequences that could have occurred.

The young officer was a quick study. She learned her lesson and had not enjoyed being prone on the ground. For the entire two years that she was in the buy team she never made the same mistake again nor did she ever not follow the directions which were given to her by her supervisor or a member of the covering team.

Chapter 4

GAME OR OPERATIONAL PLAN

If we are to single out the most important part on an undercover operation, it is my strong belief that the game plan is it. Many experienced officers could object to that statement but before you do, let me point out the reasons why I feel this way.

After having been personally involved with thousands of undercover investigations, with agencies throughout the United States and specifically in California, I have been able to sharpen and broaden my expertise in the area of undercover operations and specifically on the way in which game plans are handled and presented.

It was not too long ago that a game plan consisted of a group of officers getting together while a discussion took place regarding the imminent operation. Depending on the agency and the individual officers involved, either the supervisor or the case agent would present the planning of the operation and give out assignments.

The individual giving the information out would read, from notes which he prepared. The information given out, included but was not restricted to the location and all of the other pertinent facets of the case. The rest of the team would write down the information as it was read to them.

Different information meant different things to the officers involved and not all them would take down the same information. Because of that fact, many different agencies began to develop a game plan which was standard for undercover and similar operations within that agency.

For the most part the idea of a prepared game plan made sense, but again, different individuals and agencies would require different information and I found a very wide spectrum of game plans. Game plans on the average should be from one to three pages in length. After looking at all of the game plans from varied agencies and operations, I have put together an undercover operation game plan which should give you an idea of what I find to be the most important things that need inclusion into this form. I also strongly believe that a completed, written game

25

plan should be a mandatory part of any undercover operation. Keep in mind that the game plan I have included in this book is only a starting point. Each individual agency or officer must decide on their needs in order to develop their own plan for their individual operations.

Many supervisors and case agents feel that by including certain information in a game plan their operational ability and freedom is extremely restricted. Nothing could be farther from the truth. None of the information included in a game plan should be looked at as a restriction. The information is placed in the plan as points of reference and the parameters are set for safety reasons. Any game plan can be changed with the concurrence of the supervisor involved and the knowledge of all of the officers taking part in the operation. Let's continue with the thought process that the operational game plan is the most important part of an operation.

At the unveiling of the game plan, the officer giving out all of the information must remember that the case agent, the supervisor and the undercover operator have a lot of information on the case. The rest of the team might know something about the impending operation; however, it will be best if they are treated as officers who know nothing about the investigation. By doing this, the officer giving the briefing will give the covering team and other officers all of the pertinent facts involved in the pending operation.

Rather than go by the Game/Operation plan which I have outlined at the end of this chapter, let's try and go over the most important factors to include in any plan which is devised and the reason for doing so.

The supervisor or case agent will address the assembled team in preparation for the undercover operation.

One of the most important and often overlooked parts of a briefing is the failure to brief everyone involved at the same time. For instance, if the operation is going to utilize a patrol unit and or other officers from another agency, having a game plan including only the assigned team makes no sense. If any of the officers involved misses any part of the information being put out or if any of the officers involved is not aware of who the undercover operator or informant in the operation may be, it will be likely that during the arrest portion of the operation the officers who were briefed improperly could and would mistake the suspect for the undercover operator and informant. If this happens it could cause bodily harm to either one or both of the latter.

The briefing should begin by explaining the type of drugs and amounts or other contraband covered in the investigation.

The presentation will then move on to cover as much information as possible regarding the suspect or suspects involved in the investigation.

• Cover Background of the Suspects
• Prior Use of Guns or Acts of Violence
• Prior Arrests, Including Rap Sheet, Ncic check, Warrants, and Parole or Probation Status
• Suspects Vehicle.

If during a pre-operation surveillance, officers have seen the suspect utilize different vehicles or if officers have located the ownership of certain vehicles by the suspect, this information should be included. Also, do not neglect to mention any vehicle that the informant has seen the suspect driving or using during other encounters.

• Safety Gear. If outside personnel (officers from another agency or section) are to be involved, they must be sure to wear raid jackets and vests. If at all possible it would be advantageous to team up the outside officers with members of the team involved in the operation. If the teaming up is not possible, the assisting officers shall be supplied with radios from the agency leading the operation. There is nothing more discouraging than having someone relaying information from one frequency to another while the case unfolds.

• Deployment. There has to be a pre-arranged way for the assignment of who goes where and who does what. I have been in game plans where the supervisor has said what was to occur, without giving specific assignments, and then would say, "When I give the word all you guys come in and arrest the suspects." Imagine everybody— 10 to 15 officers— trying to get to a location first in order to take the suspect into custody. The assignments on this point have to cover the arrest team, the containment team and a team to cover the area or exits at the arrest location.

• Informant Role. After the informant is introduced to all of the officers involved in the briefing, with his role being defined, he should be excused. The investigators will then continue with the briefing. By excusing the informant from the briefing, he will not begin his schooling on the way in which law enforcement conducts undercover operations. While informants will be covered in another chapter, keep one thing in mind: Todays' informant is tomorrows' suspect.

One of the things I try to do with informants is to curtail their involvement in the operation. In other words try to get the informant out of the way as soon and as safely as possible. It is more efficient to send an informant into a situation where the officers' presence might compromise the operation or the officers' safety would be questionable.

• Money Man. If a money flash is going to be necessary it is very important for the money man, as a part time undercover operator, to know his parameters and to work out everything before hand with the main undercover operator and the supervisor. Because the money flash is the most dangerous part of the undercover operation (it will be covered in its entirety in the next chapter) it is essential that the supervisor go over all of the specific points involved.

• Monitoring the Wire. The officer who monitors the wire has to be experienced in covering undercover operators and the handling of the investigations. If the undercover operator is a close friend of someone in the squad and they, by the mere fact of working together and being close friends, have developed the ability to communicate easily, it is that individual who should monitor the wire. By having the same individual monitoring the wire, of the same operator all of the time, a working expertise is developed and the officer monitoring the wire is able to ascertain the undercover operators' need of assistance by the way in which a conversation is developing or by the way the operators' voice changes with each obstacle he confronts.

Unless the monitoring officer is overly experienced, it is advantageous to have a second individual rely the wire information to the other units. The relaying of the information will be done as the monitoring officer is listening to the wire. If the monitoring officer has to broadcast, while the conversation unfolds, he could miss important information as he talks to the covering team.

• Trouble Signals. The undercover operator shall have both a visual and a verbal signal to advise the covering team that he is in trouble. The visual signal has to be pronounced. For instance, if a suspect decides to rob the undercover operator the operator can put his hand up in the air while saying, "Don't shoot me, take the money, I'm a cop, don't hurt me." The visual signal will be his hands up in the air accompanied by the verbal sentence. The visual signal is necessary because the transmitter being carried, by the undercover operator, could and has in the past stopped working during the operation. The covering personnel can not depend on the wire all of the time. The wire is an outstanding tool but which has many limitations and pitfalls.

• Arrest Signals. Again, for the arrest to take place there must be a verbal and a visual signal. Both are necessary due to the same problems described in the trouble signal section. The visual signal for the arrest shall be implemented with a backup system. For instance, if the visual signal is for the undercover operator to remove his sun glasses upon seeing the dope, the signal might become a mute point if the undercover officer is seeing the dope after the sun goes down. The investigation could begin during the early afternoon and carry over to the evening. This would cause the undercover operator to take his glasses off permanently, prior to seeing any contraband, because of darkness. The supervisor has to make sure that there is an alternate visual signal to use in case the original signal is no longer viable. Do not make the visual signal a simple act, such as putting the operator's hand through his hair. Such a signal could be given in a very unpronounced way. This could cause the point man to miss the signal. If you coupled that with the wire not working, it is very possible that the investigators involved will miss the chance to make a timely arrest. This delay could cause problems for the undercover operator.

The verbal signal for the arrest should be short and the same each time. The reason for staying with the same word or sentence, each time, is the familiarization of those involved in the squad with the word or sentence used.

• Alternative Game Plan. If possible, the supervisor has to look at the situation and imagine what the suspect is thinking. This is a tall order, but it is a challenge that law enforcement officers must try to achieve. By doing so we could begin to anticipate any changes that the suspect would want to make as the operation unfolds. Remember that this would only be a guess and it is only discussed in order to open up a dialogue between those involved.

Speaking of dialogue, the game plan is a discussion and an exchange of ideas between the officers involved in the operation. If an operation is to be successful the supervising officer should encourage input and discussion from all involved. Likewise, if any of the officers involved feels that the plan is unsafe or that by suggesting a change the plan could become safer, he should speak up and let his feelings be known. It is much easier to have someone disagree with your input than to have an undercover operator killed or injured because one of the involved officers neglected to point out a deficiency in the plan out of fear of being challenged or made fun of.

• Undercover Vehicle. The undercover vehicle should not only be noted in the game plan but it should also be seen by all of those involved in the operation.

Do not let the undercover officer leave the briefing with a brand new vehicle which has an array of equipment that he is not familiar with. There are vehicles that have a trunk switch, a gas tank switch or other extras in remote locations. It would be very difficult to explain to a suspect that you don't know how to open the trunk, of the fancy car that you own, in order to put the dope into it.

• Radio Security. Think and believe that many suspects utilize scanners. Remember that the news media monitors police frequencies. Try to curtail the use of street names and locations. Do not broadcast the undercover operator's name over the air.

• Hospitals and Local Notifications. List the closest hospital with a trauma center. If the investigation is to take place in another jurisdiction, make sure that the watch commander is notified prior to the operation taking place.

It is important to include all of the above points in any game plan which is completed in anticipation of an undercover operation. Keep in mind that the game plan is only as restrictive as the imaginations of those involved.

Game plans and the information which is included in them is a good and very important beginning to any operation. Keep in mind that the people involved, their ability to work together, and the standard set by the supervisor in charge are all equally important.

As you can see, the importance of the game plan is unquestionable. If all of the information, covered previously, is included in the game plan and briefing, the operation will have a trouble free beginning. Everyone will know what is expected of them.

Together all of these factors complete the package. This package is the attainment of excellence in all of our endeavors.

UNDERCOVER OPERATION GAME PLAN

DATE_____ CASE AGENTS_____
TYPE AND QUANTITY OF DRUGS_____
ASSEMBLY AND BRIEFING LOCATION_____
MONEY FLASH__Y____N____BY_____LOCATION_____
BUY–BUST LOCATION_____
WIRE WORN BY_____MONITORED BY_____WIRE FREQ:_____
ARREST SIGNAL, VISUAL_____VERBAL_____
RIP SIGNAL, VISUAL_____VERBAL_____

U/C #1_____BEEPER#_____CELLULAR#_____
CLOTHING_____VEHICLE/LIC#_____
U/C #2_____BEEPER#_____CELLULAR#_____
CLOTHING_____VEHICLE/LIC#_____

C.I. #1_____BEEPER#_____CELLULAR#_____
CLOTHING_____VEHICLE/LIC#_____
C.I. #2_____BEEPER#_____CELLULAR#_____
CLOTHING_____VEHICLE/LIC#_____

SUSPECT #1_____VEHICLE_____
DESC/CLOTHING_____ARMED_____
SUSPECT #2_____VEHICLE_____
DESC/CLOTHING_____ARMED_____
SUSPECT #3_____VEHICLE_____
DESC/CLOTHING_____ARMED_____
ADDITIONAL VEHICLES, (SUSP#)_____
RAP SHEET ATTACHED, SUSPECT #1____Y____N____,SUSPECT
#2____Y____N____, SUSPECT #3____Y____N____.

PERSONNEL

OFFICER	UNIT	VEHICLE	OFFICER	UNIT	VEHICLE

OUTSIDE PERSONNEL INVOLVED.____Y____N____.
NOTIFICATIONS: WATCH COMMANDER, (NAME AND DEPART-
MENT):_____
NOTIFIED BY_____TIME_____UNIFORM OFFICERS DEPLOYED.
NAMES AND UNIT NUMBERS_____
LOCATION OF SUSPECTS BOOKING_____
TRANSPORTATION OF SUSPECTS_____
_____

SPECIAL ASSIGNMENTS:

SURVEILLANCE UNITS_____
_____

U/C OFFICER COVER TEAM_____
OTHER:_____
_____

NEAREST HOSPITAL: EMERGENCY ROOM PHONE #_____
NAME AND ADDRESS_____
OPERATION PLAN:_____
_____
_____
_____
_____
_____
_____
_____

DATE AND TIME OF ARREST_____
SUPERVISOR AT SCENE_____

Chapter 5

MONEY FLASH

Before we start to discuss money flashes I would like to make a very important point. The first thing to attempt, on an undercover buy, would be to do the deal without showing any money. An undercover operator is really experienced and knows how to control the buy when he is able to do it without showing any money. The case agent, the supervisor and the operator can use their imaginations and expertise in selling this point to the suspects with whom they are dealing.

Many undercover operators have died due to mismanagement of the flash roll. Narcotics traffickers become involved in the dealing of narcotics in order to amass large amounts of currency. This goal is attained by selling the narcotics to buyers or by simply ripping the buyers off. The suspect will not think twice about ripping the buyer off if he perceives that the rip off could be undertaken relatively easy. Keep the word PERCEPTION in mind. This word will play an important part in the management of the flash roll.

The most dangerous part of any undercover operation is when the money is flashed to the suspect and when the narcotics are shown to the undercover operator. The reason for the heightened sense of danger is due to the fact that it is at this time that both sides are waiting for the rip off, or in the case of the dealer, the arrest to occur.

As the deal develops, the suspect will begin a process by which he will decide whether he will in fact exchange the narcotics for the currency or rip the currency off from the undercover operator. At this point in the operation the suspect does not believe that the undercover operator is anything other than a criminal. He would not continue dealing with an individual he believed to be a cop. The suspect has a very important thing in mind: his freedom. He will be happy to either sell the narcotics for the currency or rip the currency off while retaining his narcotics but his freedom is most important.

The suspect knows that he also runs a risk of being ripped off. He knows that his greatest risk, to be ripped off, is when he shows the

33

undercover operator his narcotics. At that time the suspect will have a fully alert posture and will be poised to defend his wares and or himself in case of an attack.

Sometimes the suspect will show his narcotics to the undercover operator prior to the flashing of the undercover roll. In today's climate it is becoming more difficult for the suspect to show the narcotics without a money flash.

Many undercover operators become relaxed after the flash of the money has occurred. This type of feeling could be equated to being complacent and that is a word that undercover operators can not entertain. The undercover operator must remain alert and mentally prepared, especially immediately following the money flash and prior to seeing the dope.

When the undercover operator and the suspect begin to negotiate for the flash to take place, it is important to ascertain if the suspect wants to count the money prior to the exchange. I have found that most narcotic dealers will not attempt to count the money at first. They will look through the flash roll and will be satisfied with the money as it is shown. The counting of the money becomes a negotiating factor. For instance, the undercover operator can tell the suspect that he can see the money but he, the undercover operator, wants to see the dope before the counting of the currency takes place. This does not mean that we will never let the suspect count the money. Anything is possible as long as it is controlled by the officers running the operation. This will go a long way in guaranteeing the safety of those involved.

Many undercover operators get involved in complex negotiations with the suspect, such as requesting a quantitative test of the narcotics. One thing is sure, the more sophisticated the undercover operator gets with the suspect, the more the suspect will demand from the undercover operator when his time is up. This also holds true during the planning of the money flash. If the undercover officer has five hired guns at the location where the flash is taking place, such as a hotel room or any other location, that undercover operator better expect the same type of security to take place during the viewing of the dope.

Let's get back to the word PERCEPTION. It really does not matter what we think about the plan or how well we think the undercover operator is being covered. What really matters is what the suspect perceives as the flash and further negotiations are taking place. For example, the undercover operator is flashing one million dollars to a suspect inside a hotel room. The undercover operator knows that the two rooms adjacent to his room contain numerous officers who are ready to respond to his aid if necessary.

The suspect walks into the undercover room and sees one million dollars for him to count. He does not know about the officers in the adjacent rooms. The only person he sees in the room is the undercover operator. The suspect perceives, rightfully so, that the only person and obstacle between him and one million dollars is the undercover operator.

At this time the suspect will decide what action to take. If he decides to rip off the money and to kill the undercover operator in the process, there is nothing that all of those officers next door can do. Remember, we can only react to an action by the suspect, we are not proactive at this point in the operation. There is no doubt that the money will be safe, the suspect will not leave the room with the money. The undercover operator will have been harmed, by the suspect, prior to the entry of the covering team into the undercover room.

Everyone knows that undercover operations (especially the money flash) are very dangerous investigations. Many officers subscribe to the belief that the risk undertaken in undercover operations is part of the job and there is nothing anyone can do to change that fact. In other words, "that's part of the price we pay for doing this type of business." Officers with that frame of mind should find alternative types of work. It is not necessary to run a great risk while flashing currency during an undercover operation.

While there is always a risk and danger involved in any money flash situation, proper planning and execution of the plan goes a long way in guaranteeing the safety of those involved.

Again, I will go over numerous ways in which to do a safe money flash. There could be other variations of the flash that many officers are aware of. I only list these points as a starting reference. Money flashes, as any other part of the undercover operation, are as restrictive as the imagination of those involved and the different policies of the different agencies.

• Do not use the money flash as a tool to entice the suspect into the deal. When the undercover operator the case agent or the supervisor begin to look at the money flash as an object rather than the true value of the money involved, the safety process begins to unravel. If the "object" rather than "money" mentality is allowed to continue, the case will deteriorate and the safety of those involved will be jeopardized.

• Do not do a flash unless the suspect asks to see the money. Undercover operators should negotiate with the suspect in an attempt to see the dope, prior to having the flash take place.

• If the suspect requests to see the money I would, personally, like to do most money flashes as a surprise flash. Do the flash when the suspect is not expecting it. For instance if the suspect wants to meet in order to talk about the deal, take that occasion to do the flash. The suspect will have no idea that he is about to see the money. The undercover operator will pick the location of the meet. After the flash the undercover operator can tell the suspect that he is ready to deal. Since the suspect has already seen the money the undercover operator can demand to see the dope prior to having the suspect count the money and the exchange taking place.

• Any time a flash is undertaken, law enforcement should have a ratio of two to three officers per suspect. Only one suspect sees the money. There is no need for more than one suspect to be taken to a location where the flash will take place. This holds true whether the flash is to be conducted indoors or in an outside location.

• There are some points that the undercover operator has to entertain if the flash is handled as a surprise flash. For instance, the undercover operator has to be sure that he is not dealing with a broker who has no control of the dope. If the money is shown prematurely to a broker, during early negotiations, it is likely that later on when the main suspect enters the picture he would request to see the money again. While I never say never, on undercover operations, it will be very unlikely that I will entertain doing a second money flash during a dope deal. For those who entertain doing a second money flash, keep this in mind, do not handle the second flash in the same manner or location where the first flash took place. By this time, the suspect is aware of how the first flash went down and if he has a rip off in mind, the only way to avoid it is by catching the suspect off guard on the second flash.

• The second point that the undercover operator has to realize is that after seeing the money, in a surprise flash, the suspect could decide to show the undercover operator a portion of the dope rather than the whole amount. The suspect will tell the undercover operator that he will show part of the dope as an act of good faith and that the rest of the dope will be shown once the money is counted and at the scene of the final meet. At that point the undercover operator and the covering team should have a plan in place to either terminate the operation by arresting the suspect, with the amount of dope he has shown, or demand that the suspect bring out the whole amount before the money moves. Again it depends on the individuals involved.

• The new undercover operators can get their best schooling in how to protect the flash roll by observing the way in which narcotics dealers protect their narcotics.

• The undercover operator must not place himself in a position to get kidnapped by the suspect. Let's say that the operator does a surprise flash on the suspect and the money is then driven away from the flash scene. After the money leaves, the undercover operator tells the suspect that once he, the undercover operator, sees the dope all he has to do is call the money back to the location. The suspect PERCEIVES that the undercover operator has all of the control in the movement of the money. While the covering team knows different, knowing that we will not have any additional flash, this fact means nothing. The suspect will act on his PERCEPTION of what is occurring. If the suspect is going to rip off the undercover operator, all he has to do is to get the undercover operator into a situation which the suspect controls. For instance, the suspect could get the undercover operator to sit in his vehicle, hold a gun to the operators' head and order him to call the money back. The operator could be told to use a cellular phone. This would preclude the operator from leaving the car at all.

The officers who plan the operation can avoid this scenario by undertaking a simple step. The undercover operator has to tell the suspect that the money will not return unless the following occurs: 1) the undercover operator has to see the dope. 2) The undercover operator will have to be standing by himself at a prearranged location. The owner of the money will continue to drive by that location for the next 20 minutes. If the owner does not see the undercover operator standing at the location, alone, he will leave the area taking the money with him. This part will be an easy sell if the undercover operator portrayed himself as a broker. If he did not, it will be a little harder to sell.

• If the undercover operator wants to get real fancy, he could utilize an airplane or a boat to do the flash. All of the individuals in the plane or the boat will be covering officers and the suspect will be patted down for weapons upon his arrival at the location of departure. Using either a plane or boat is restricted to major type operations. Do not use a conveyance of this type while you negotiate to buy 2 kilos of coke. The game does not fit the amount!

• Remember the flash roll will be moved as soon as possible, if not immediately, after it is flashed. Again, do not forget PERCEPTIONS. To move the money, without letting the suspect know that it is moved, is no accomplishment. If the suspect thinks that the money is still within his reach, the undercover operator is still at risk.

• After flashing the money do not get into your car with the suspect in order to travel to a second location. This is especially important if the same vehicle contains the money which was flashed to the suspect. The operator could travel with the suspect if the money has been removed and the suspect is unable to get the money moved.

• Individuals in law enforcement believe that by using a restrictive location such as a hotel room, an apartment, a house or any other type of dwelling, we can conduct a safer undercover operation. The fact is that by using any type of enclosed location the planners of an operation overlook many of the pitfalls of using such locations.

This is true because the covering team falls into a false sense of security. The covering team feels that by having the undercover room covered with personnel in the adjoining rooms the suspect will not be able to harm the undercover operator.

The suspect knows nothing about the covering team. If he did, he would not be hanging around.

I'm not saying not to use a dwelling while you do a dope deal. If you do, place the safety emphasis on the people inside the undercover room. The same rules apply inside as it does when doing business in an open place.

Use two or more undercover officers at the location. Always have two or three times the ratio of officers to suspects. If the suspect wants to rip the undercover operator off, he has to figure out how to kill two or more people instead of one. The undercover officers should sit at separate locations inside the room. This causes a split situation for the suspect as he is making his plans. More than likely he will abort any attempt at ripping the undercover officers. The suspect knows that he will be unable to shoot two or more undercover operators at the same time. The suspects' safety becomes an issue—a very important issue to him.

• When all else fails, lie. There is no law or policy that says undercover operators can not lie to the suspects. The suspects lie to us all of the time. We can do the same.

• The supervisor is the individual responsible for the safety of the flash and ultimately the safety of all the officers involved. The supervisor must understand flash management and has to be prepared to correct any deficiencies or terminate the case, at a moment's notice. The supervisor shall not sacrifice any of the safety aspects of the operation in the quest to seize narcotics or other contraband. To do so will be to sentence one of his subordinates to death.

From past experience the red flags, which were stated before, have become very obvious during undercover operations. Those flags will alert any knowledgeable supervisor of possible disaster. If detected, those flags will cause the supervisor to change the course of the operation or complete termination of the operation.

Use your knowledge and leadership ability and the operation will be fruitful and successful.

Money Management Compromises

As I stated at the beginning of this chapter, many undercover officers have died as a result of poor flash roll management. I would like to relate two cases that will exemplify that fact. The first case occurred to members of the Los Angeles Police Department. The second case occurred in Southern California to members of another agency.

In 1973 the Major Violators Section of Narcotics Division, Los Angeles Police Department, received information from an informant, stating that a suspect was interested in dealing a large quantity of cocaine.

The informant was willing to introduce an undercover operator to the suspect. The supervisor in charge of the operation asked to use an undercover officer from another squad. An undercover officer by the name of Blackie Sawyer was given the assignment.

After debriefing the informant, Blackie set up a date to go to the suspect's house and flash $50,000, the price of the cocaine. The informant and Blackie went to the suspect's residence and the flash took place. While Blackie sat outside, in the undercover vehicle, the informant was inside the house talking to the main suspect. The main suspect had sent a second suspect to the car to look at the money.

The main suspect told the informant that he was not willing to deal any dope, to the undercover operator, that evening. In the ensuing conversation the suspect told the informant that he had a new shipment of cocaine coming in. The informant told the suspect that his man, the undercover operator, had $140,000 at his disposal to buy cocaine. The suspect upped the deal from the original figure to 4 kilos of cocaine. The total cost of the new deal would be $140,000.

The informant exited the house and returned to the undercover vehicle. He advised the undercover operator of the sudden change. Blackie was not very happy about the way in which the flash took place. He was also concerned that the suspect had raised the amount of cocaine to be purchased. This had all taken place without Blackie's input.

The following day, Blackie brought forward his concerns to his supervisor and requested that his partner, P. Kearney, be allowed to assist him in the case as a second undercover operator.

The suspect, who was being targeted, was very well documented both by the L.A.P.D. and by the D.E.A.

During a meeting with all of the personnel involved, Blackie's supervisor brought up Blackie's concerns to the supervisor running the case. (Remember, the case was being run by another squad, Blackie was assisting because of his undercover expertise.) The supervisor in charge of the case decided against using a second undercover operator. His reasoning was that he did not want to scare the suspect away by introducing a new face into the case.

At this time Blackie was given the option of backing out of the operation. Blackie decided to remain as the undercover operator and go at it solo.

A second meet between Blackie, the informant and one of the suspects took place. This meet did not produce any results. The informant spoke to the main suspect and he set up the deal to go down to a hotel in Santa Monica.

The plan was for the suspect or one of his cohorts to meet Blackie in the lobby of the hotel. After a short conversation Blackie would take the suspect into the undercover room to count the money.

The deal was set up with the undercover room in the middle of two adjoining rooms, each containing covering team personnel. The officers in one of the rooms had access to the undercover room via an adjoining door. It was in this room that the wire was being monitored.

Note: A few days prior to the meet at the hotel in Santa Monica, surveilling units had followed one of the suspects to a gun shop and had verified that he had purchased a small caliber semi-automatic handgun. Also prior to the last meet and during the negotiations, the main suspect had threatened the informant by placing a .45 caliber pistol under his chin and telling him that if he or his partner were cops he would kill them both. The suspect removed the pistol from the informant's chin and fired one round through a window in the house. The suspect fired the weapon in order to make his point known to the informant.

Let's stop for a minute and look at the red flags. 1) The suspect ups the deal for no apparent reason. As a matter of course, most suspects want to start dealing small and graduate to larger amounts of dope. They do this to verify that they are not dealing with cops or criminals who are going to rip them off. 2) Blackie had a bad feeling about the case and asked for a second undercover operator. 3) The covering team and the supervisor were aware of the propensity for violence. This was manifested by the main suspect's threat to the informant and the fact that a second suspect purchased a small caliber pistol and ammunition prior to the last meet. 4) The undercover operator had not seen any dope up to that time. The decision was made to flash $140,000 to the suspects, a second flash, without making a demand to see some dope.

During the game planning stages it became clear to everyone involved that there was no way that the suspect, in the undercover room, would be able to leave that room carrying the flash money. The plan to stop the theft of the money was outstanding but the safety of the undercover operator was overlooked. This is obvious from what has transpired so far in the investigation.

With everyone in place the informant placed a call to the suspect. Instead of having the suspect meet Blackie in the lobby of the hotel, as previously planned, the informant told the suspect the number of the undercover room.

After the informant hung up the phone, Blackie turned to the supervisor and requested to have his partner, Kearny, in the room with him as a safety valve. Blackie was concerned about the undercover room having been compromised. The request was denied. Blackie then asked to move the room to another location. That request was also denied. The supervisor did not want to scare the suspect away with any changes.

Again, red flags or danger signals became very obvious, the mind set continued to be full speed ahead, everything was under control. Even though there was officers everywhere and everything was covered, the direction which the case was taking was being controlled by the suspects in the case.

In fact, the suspects in this case have a lot more control than they knew. They knew where the money was to be flashed and they would be able to communicate with each other via the telephone if necessary.

The covering units took their positions and the informant along with Blackie awaited the suspects arrival.

A short time later a suspect arrived at the hotel and went up to the undercover room. This would be the same suspect who had purchased the small caliber pistol and had been seen practicing on his draw and shooting techniques.

The suspect entered the room and began counting the money. As it usually happens, the wire became inoperative. The covering team in the room next door moved towards the adjoining door and began to listen through the door.

After counting the money once, the suspect told the informant and Blackie that the count was short. The phone inside the undercover room rang and Blackie answered it. The calling party hung up.

The units who were surveilling the main suspect, Boyle, observed him to be at a phone booth across the street from the hotel making phone calls.

Boyle called the room and spoke to his partner in crime. After a short conversation the suspect gave the phone to the informant. Boyle was advised by the informant that there would be a second money count, since the suspect screwed up the first count.

The phone conversation terminated and the suspect inside the under-cover room began to count the money a second time.

NOTE: As matter of experience suspects who plan to rip the under-cover officers count the money more than once. This is done because they are trying to get their nerve up in order to carry out the rip. Most suspects do not request to do a dollar by dollar count prior to showing dope.

After the count was completed, on the second try, the amount was correct. The informant got up and told the suspect that he wanted to go see the dope. The suspect told the informant that he wanted to go to the bathroom before leaving.

The suspect entered the bathroom, exited after a short time and began to walk towards the front door.

PERCEPTION. What did the suspect perceive? He perceived that between himself and $140,000 there was only one person—Blackie. The informant was a non-factor in the deal. So by killing Blackie the suspect knew that he could walk out of the room with the money. The covering team knew different. They knew that the suspect would not leave the room with the money, but they would be unable to stop the suspect from taking the first step in his quest to rip off Blackie. They were reactive at this time in the deal.

As soon as the suspect reached the front door of the room, and without any warning, he drew a small caliber pistol and began shooting at Blackie. Blackie drew his revolver from the small of his back and returned fire. Blackie missed his mark. The suspect's first shot entered Blackie's left side severing his aorta.

The covering team entered the undercover room. The first officer to enter, exchanged shots with the suspect. Neither was hit. As the entry was made, before the point officer could take a second shot, the officers to the rear went after the suspect. By doing this they knocked down the only individual who had a clear shot at the suspect. The covering officers took the suspect into custody without incident. Boyle was arrested without incident at the phone booth across from the hotel. Blackie died at the hotel room as a result of his wound.

The decisions made in this case were made with the best intentions in mind. The supervisors felt that they had all of the angles covered. At the time, the investigators involved did not have the training and/or experience that their peers have today. Keep one thing in mind; cases like this are being undertaken daily all over the nation by well-meaning narcotics investigators with little or not experience in the field of undercover work.

NOTE: The suspects were tried for murder in Santa Monica, California. They were found not guilty. The defense attorney used the defense of self-defense in the shooting, telling the jury that Blackie drew his weapon first and that the suspect fired back in order to defend himself. The jury bought it. The informant was a terrible witness. Blackie was the only other individual who could have said what really happened in the undercover room but he was dead.

The second case which I will relay to you is more recent and also happened in Southern California. The individuals involved were members of numerous law enforcement entities, both local and federal, working a task force.

The undercover officers negotiated to buy a pound of china white heroin from a suspect who was from Thailand. On the day of the deal three undercover officers met the suspect at a restaurant and flashed him the money. After the flash went down the suspect told the undercover officers that he would go with them, in their car, to the house where the dope was. The suspect requested that the undercover officers take the $80,000 flash with them to that location.

NOTE: This would be my first red flag on this case. 1.) the suspect is willing to take the buyers to the stash pad, 2.) he would travel with the undercover officers in their car along with the flash roll. Maybe the three undercover officers and the supervisor thought that three against one was real good odds; however, the way to manage the roll has to be undertaken from the perspective of what the suspect perceives and what his plans are, rather than the numbers or the odds involved. In this case the suspect is telling the operators what to do, where and when . . .

The covering team, who were surveilling during the meet and ensuing movements, observed a vehicle in the same parking lot where the flash was taking place. The vehicle contained two young Orientals who were really interested in the area where the undercover officers were meeting with the main suspect.

The suspect entered the undercover vehicle and they drove away. As the surveillance continued, the surveilling officers again observed the same vehicle, which they had seen in the parking lot, following the undercover operators and the main suspect.

One of the local officers ran the license of the vehicle containing the two young Orientals. It returned to a stolen vehicle.

NOTE: This is not a red flag, this is an atomic explosion. I do not believe that dope dealers undertake dope deals while driving stolen vehicles. As a matter of course they want as little notice from law enforcement as possible and they do not attain this by driving a stolen car. Without being a Monday morning quarterback, there is no doubt in my mind that I would have stopped the deal at this time.

The supervisor running the case was advised of the fact that the vehicle, following the undercover operators, was a stolen vehicle. The officers giving that information to the supervisor told him that they had communications with a local unit and they could request to have that vehicle stopped.

The supervisor replied not to do so. He was afraid that if the second vehicle was stopped and if that vehicle was, in fact, involved in the deal, the stop would cause the deal to come to an end. The supervisor decided to let the case continue.

NOTE: At this time the supervisor had lost sight of his real responsibility. That responsibility is the safety and well being of his officers. The supervisor placed the deal ahead of the safety of the officers involved.

The surveillance continued and the suspect in the undercover vehicle had the officers stop on a residential street which was very desolate and hard to cover by surveilling units. The second vehicle also stopped but the two occupants remained inside.

All that the surveilling units could do was to drive by and give information over the radio while they had the undercover vehicle in sight. The street was hilly so it was not too long of a drive until the surveillance units lost sight of the undercover vehicle. To top it all, the supervisor had been caught in traffic and was some distance away from the scene. The surveilling units did not like the way in which the case was shaping up and asked the supervisor if they could terminate it. The supervisor told the units to await his arrival before taking any action.

The main suspect exited the undercover vehicle and began to walk up a driveway of a residence, as he did so, the vehicle with the two other suspects had moved closer. Both suspects exited and were approaching the undercover vehicle with guns drawn.

The undercover officers were not aware of the second car or the suspects approaching from behind.

The suspect who had been inside the undercover vehicle stopped and returned to talk to the undercover officers.

The main suspect drew a handgun and demanded that the undercover officers give him the money. By that time the other two suspects were next to the undercover vehicle covering, the undercover officers with handguns.

The undercover officer sitting in the back seat of the car told the main suspect that he would give him the money and not to hurt them. The suspect told the undercover officer that he was not going to hurt them, he only wanted the money. The undercover officer gave the suspect the money and the suspect began shooting.

Surveillance units were aware, by this time, of the situation and were doing the best they could to stop harm from coming to the undercover officers. The ensuing shootout between the surveilling units and the suspects resulted in the death of two of the three suspects. The third suspect was shot numerous times but lived. He was later convicted.

All three of the undercover officers were shot. One lived, the other two died as a result of their wounds.

There is nothing that can be said about any officer, especially an undercover officer, who is killed in the line of duty.

One thing is sure, THERE IS NO CONTRABAND OR MONEY WORTH THE LIFE OF ANY LAW ENFORCEMENT OFFICER. DO NOT JEOPARDIZE YOUR FAMILY OR YOUR FINANCIAL STABILITY.

Chapter 6

OPERATIONS LIST

I will include a set of lists that can be utilized by officers, undertaking undercover operations. These points are only to be considered as a beginning point. The individual officers and agencies should expand the entries in order to include their own needs.

Planning the Operation

1. BACKGROUND OF SUSPECTS.
   A. PRIOR USE OF: GUNS, ACTS OF VIOLENCE.
   B. PRIOR ARRESTS: RAP SHEETS, NCIC CHECKS, WARRANT CHECKS ETC.
   C. KNOWN VEHICLES (S): DESCRIPTIONS, DMV CHECKS.
2. LICENSE NUMBERS:
   D. PHOTOS OF SUSPECTS, ASSOCIATES.
   E. ADDITIONAL INFORMATION.
3. DETAILED GAME PLAN.
   A. EMERGENCY INFORMATION: HOSPITAL LOCATION, PHONE NUMBERS TO EMERGENCY ROOM.
   B. LOCAL LAW ENFORCEMENT PHONE NUMBERS.
4. BRIEFING OF ALL CONCERNED PERSONNEL.
   A. EVERYONE HAS TO BE BRIEFED AT THE SAME TIME.
5. UNDERCOVER OFFICER AND INFORMANT.
   A. IDENTIFIED TO EVERYONE PARTICIPATING IN THE OPERATION. (THIS INCLUDES PATROL OFFICERS ASSIGNED TO ASSIST AT THE TIME OF ARREST).
6. OUTSIDE PERSONNEL.
   A. IDENTIFY TO EVERYONE PARTICIPATING IN THE OPERATION. PROVIDE RAID JACKETS AND VESTS IF NECESSARY. TEAM UP WITH LOCAL OFFICERS. EXCHANGE RADIOS.

7. DEPLOYMENT.
   A. WHO DOES WHAT. WHO GOES WHERE. MAKE THE ASSIGNMENTS.
8. ROLE OF THE INFORMANT.
9. MONEY MAN UNDERCOVER OFFICER.
   A. DEFINE HIS ROLE.
10. MONITORING OF WIRE.
    A. TEST THE WIRE FIRST THING IN THE FIELD.
    B. IF POSSIBLE, THE WIRE SHOULD BE MONITORED BY THE SAME OFFICER ON ALL INVESTIGATIONS, USING THE SAME OPERATOR. THE MONITOR GETS TO KNOW THE OPERATOR'S VOICE AND METHODS OF OPERATION.
    C. USE ANOTHER OFFICER TO BROADCAST. THE OFFICER MONITORING THE WIRE CANNOT DO BOTH. TWO CARS SIDE BY SIDE CAN DO THE JOB.
11. SIGNALS—AUDIO AND VISUAL.
    A. USE SAME SIGNAL FOR ARREST IN EVERY CASE.
    B. USE SAME WORD FOR TROUBLE IN EVERY CASE.
    C. VISUAL SIGNALS WILL HAVE TO BE CHANGED TO MEET TIME OF DAY, WEATHER CONDITIONS, ETC. TRY TO USE SAME SIGNAL WHEN POSSIBLE.
12. ALTERNATIVE GAME PLANS.
    A. TRY TO LOOK AT THE SITUATION THROUGH THE SUSPECT'S EYES. THINK OF ACCEPTABLE REACTIONS TO SUSPECT'S ANTICIPATED GAME PLAN.
    B. SUPERVISOR IN CHARGE SET PARAMETERS FOR THE OPERATOR. ONCE THE OPERATOR GOES OUTSIDE THOSE PARAMETERS, THE CASE IS OVER.
13. UNDERCOVER VEHICLE.
    A. ALL PERSONNEL FAMILIAR WITH THE VEHICLE TO BE USED.
    B. OPERATOR HAS TO BE FAMILIAR WITH THE VEHICLE—HOW TO MAKE THINGS WORK, TRUNK OPENING, WINDOWS ETC.
14. RADIO SECURITY.
    A. THINK SCANNERS. SUSPECTS HAVE THEM, NEWS MEDIA HAVE THEM AND ALL OF THE POLICE BAND BUFFS.
    B. DO NOT USE THE OPERATOR'S NAME OVER THE AIR.

15. RIP OFFS POSSIBLE INDICATORS.
    A. SUSPECTS SELLING DOPE TOO CHEAP.
    B. SUSPECTS DEMAND THAT THE TRANSACTION TAKE PLACE IN A LOCATION OF THEIR CONTROL, (I.E. A PRIVATE RESIDENCE, BUSINESS OR MOTEL ROOM).
    C. SUSPECTS INSIST ON HAVING ADDITIONAL MANPOWER DURING THE MONEY FLASH.
    D. AFTER ONE MONEY COUNT, THE SUSPECTS REQUEST TO COUNT THE MONEY AGAIN.
    E. SUSPECTS INSIST THAT THE OPERATOR BRING THE MONEY ALONE.
    F. SUSPECTS CHANGE THE GAME PLAN MID–STREAM AND ATTEMPT TO COAX THE OPERATOR AND THE MONEY TO ANOTHER LOCATION. NORMALLY TO AN ISOLATED AREA. (REMEMBER THE OPERATOR IS A BUSINESS MAN. HE HAS TO PROTECT THE MONEY AND INSIST ON A NEUTRAL LOCATION, PREFERABLY AN OPEN AREA IN PUBLIC VIEW).
    G. ONE OR MORE OF THE SUSPECTS ARE DRIVING A STOLEN VEHICLE. THESE SUSPECTS DO NOT WANT TO BRING ATTENTION TO THEMSELVES. BY DRIVING A STOLEN VEHICLE THEY ARE GIVING YOU A NOTICE THAT THEY ARE PLANNING TO RIP YOU OFF.
    H. UNEXPECTED ADDITIONAL SUSPECTS (ARMED OR OTHERWISE) APPEAR DURING THE MONEY FLASH.

PLAN FOR THE WORST ON EVERY UNDERCOVER OPERATION. COVER ALL ASPECTS OF THE GAME AS IF YOU HAVE PRIOR KNOWLEDGE THAT THE SUSPECTS WILL ATTEMPT A RIP OFF.

NEVER, AT ANY TIME, DO YOU ALLOW THE SUSPECTS TO BELIEVE THAT THEY HAVE EITHER PHYSICAL OR PSYCHOLOGICAL CONTROL OVER THE TRANSACTION.

Preparing for the Undercover Role

1. GO OVER THE QUESTIONS THAT ARISE BETWEEN THE OPERATOR AND THE SUSPECT.
    A. THINK AND TALK THROUGH THE OPERATION TO YOURSELF: TRY TO THINK LIKE A DOPE DEALER AND

HAVE THE ANSWERS FOR QUESTIONS YOU EXPECT THE SUSPECT TO ASK.

B. SIT DOWN WITH A SUPERVISOR, PARTNER OR ANOTHER OPERATOR AND "WHAT IF" THE HELL OUT OF THE CASE.

C. IF YOU HAVE ANY QUESTIONS, DO NOT BE AFRAID TO ASK THEM. DO NOT LET YOUR EGO GET IN THE WAY OF YOUR SAFETY.

D. PLAN ALL ASPECTS OF THE CASE. DO NOT ASSUME THAT SOMEONE ELSE WILL TAKE CARE OF THE DETAILS.

2. CLOTHING.

A. SHOULD BE COMFORTABLE.

B. FIT INTO THE SITUATION, YOUR ROLE AND THE AREA.

3. FALSE I. D.

A. HAVE READY. KNOW WHAT IT SAYS.

4. WEAPON.

A. HAVE ONE. SUSPECTS USUALLY DO. HAVE IT ACCESSIBLE.

5. PHONE NUMBER.

A. HAVE A NUMBER YOU CAN GIVE THE SUSPECTS.

6. KNOW ABOUT THE DOPE YOU ARE BUYING.

A. THE SUSPECT WILL KNOW.

B. KNOW THE PRICES.

C. KNOW HOW TO TEST IT.

D. HOW PACKAGED.

E. HOW IT IS USED.

7. IF WORKING WITH INFORMANT.

A. MAKE SURE THE INFORMANT DOES NOT GIVE A STORY WHICH YOU CAN NOT COVER. DEBRIEF HIM.

B. MAKE SURE YOU HAVE ALL OF THE INFORMATION THAT THE INFORMANT CAN PROVIDE.

8. MAKE EXCUSE IN ADVANCE FOR NOT USING DOPE.

A. MEDICAL PROBLEM—HIGH BLOOD PRESSURE, HEART TROUBLE, BROKEN NOSE, ALLERGIC REACTION.

B. HAVE BEEN A VICTIM OF RIP OFF SO YOU DO NOT WANT TO GET HIGH.

C. ON PROBATION OR PAROLE—EXPECTING TO BE TEST-

ED BY PAROLE/PROBATION OFFICER (REMEMBER TO KNOW A PRISON IF YOU ARE GOING TO USE PAROLE AS AN EXCUSE).

9. HAVE A PLAN TO ESCAPE OR BE RESCUED IF SOMETHING GOES WRONG.
   A. FAKE A HEART ATTACK, SEIZURE, ETC.
   B. HAVE PRE-ARRANGED SIGNAL FOR RIP-OFF, GUNS BEING SEEN, NEW SUSPECTS OR TERMINATION OF THE OPERATION.
   C. HAVE A PRE-ARRANGED LOCATION TO ESCAPE AND MEET.
   D. KNOW WHAT YOU WILL DO IN FACE OF IMMINENT DEATH THREAT BY SUSPECTS. IDENTIFY YOURSELF AS A POLICE OFFICER WHEN FACED WITH A THREAT. TRY TO CALM THE SUSPECT DOWN AND MAKE SURE HE UNDERSTANDS YOU ARE WIRED; BACK UP OFFICERS ARE COVERING YOU AND WILL BE RESPONDING IMMEDIATELY. DO NOT ESCALATE THE SITUATION UNLESS YOU CANNOT AVOID IT.

10. UNDERSTAND THE BOUNDARIES OF THE CASE AS SET BY THE SUPERVISOR.
    A. WHERE YOU CAN AND CANNOT GO.
    B. KNOW THE AREA.

During the Operation

1. ELECTRONICS.
   A. CHECK THE BODY WIRE AT EVERY OPPORTUNITY. LET THE OPERATOR KNOW IT IS WORKING.
   B. BODY WIRE IS THE OPERATOR'S LIFELINE TO BACK UP; HE SHOULD TALK TO MONITORING OFFICERS OVER THE WIRE EVERY CHANCE HE GETS.
   C. ASSIGN AN OFFICER TO LET THE OPERATOR KNOW THAT THE WIRE IS NOT WORKING. HAVE A SIGNAL, I. E. FINGER TO EAR.
   D. KNOW BATTERY LIFE OF YOUR EQUIPMENT. IF OPERATION WILL GO LONGER THAN BATTERY LIFE, CARRY EXTRA BATTERY.

     E. ASSUME THAT BODY WIRE IS OUT OF ORDER DURING NEGOTIATIONS.

2. MEETING WITH SUSPECTS.
   A. REMEMBER THEY WANT TO SELL DOPE.
   B. PUT THEM AT EASE. SELL YOURSELF. TRY TO GET THE CROOKS TO LIKE YOU AND RESPECT YOU.
   C. DO NOT ACT LIKE A BAD ASS KILLER, BE FRIENDLY. DO NOT ACT LIKE A NERD. BE A BUSINESSMAN WHO WILL PACK UP AND LEAVE IF THE DEAL STARTS TO GO WRONG.
   D. PICK UP A MEET LOCATION THAT WILL BE EASY TO COVER.
   E. DO NOT SIT AROUND AND DRINK. IF THERE IS A DELAY, GET AWAY FROM THE SUSPECTS.
   F. USE INFORMANTS FOR DANGEROUS SITUATIONS.

3. NEGOTIATING THE DEAL.
   A. UNDERCOVER OFFICER DOES NOT RUN THE CASE ONCE HE IS UNDERCOVER.
   B. EXCEPTION. HE CAN CALL THE CASE OFF IF HE DOES NOT FEEL RIGHT ABOUT SOMETHING.
   C. MOST IMPORTANT—COMPLETE DEAL SAFELY.
   D. OPERATOR HAS TO REMEMBER THAT HIS ACTIONS, WHILE UNDERCOVER, CREATE A REACTION BY COVERING TROOPS. THINK OF THE PROBLEMS YOU MIGHT CAUSE THE COVERING OFFICERS, BEFORE GOING OFF HALF COCKED.
   E. COMPLETE THE DEAL ON OUR TERMS; BE FLEXIBLE ENOUGH WITH THE SUSPECTS TO COMPLETE THE DEAL; REMEMBER THE PRIOR PARAMETERS SET.
   F. SAMPLE BUYS HAVE TO GO DOWN IN THE SAME WAY THAT YOU WOULD CONDUCT THE MAIN DEAL.
   G. DO NOT CLAIM OWNERSHIP OF THE MONEY. THIS GIVES YOU AN EXCUSE TO USE THE PHONE IN ORDER TO CALL THE OWNER OF THE MONEY. IT ALSO GIVES YOU A CHANCE TO BACK OUT DUE TO THE PRESSURES PUT ON BY THE OWNER. THE BOTTOM LINE IS THAT IT BUYS YOU TIME IF NECESSARY.

4. MONEY FLASH.
   A. THIS IS THE POINT OF GREATEST DANGER.

B. WHEN IT COMES TO FLASHING MONEY, THINK LIKE A DOPE DEALER.

C. AVOID THINKING OF THE MONEY AS A TOOL.

D. NEVER SHOW THE MONEY WHERE THE SUSPECT THINKS HE IS IN CONTROL. IF THE SUSPECT IS PLANNING A RIP OFF HE SHOULD THINK THAT THE TIMING IS BAD. THE SUSPECT WILL THINK THAT THE NEXT TIME WILL BE BETTER. OF COURSE THERE WILL NOT BE A NEXT TIME.

E. SHOW THE MONEY TO ONE SUSPECT ONLY.

F. ALWAYS TWO OR MORE COPS ON ONE SUSPECT.

G. ALWAYS TRY A SURPRISE FLASH.

H. AVOID FLASHING THE MONEY TWICE.

I. AFTER THE MONEY IS FLASHED, MOVE THE MONEY; IF THIS IS NOT POSSIBLE, SECURE THE MONEY IN SUCH A MANNER THAT A RIP OFF IS NOT POSSIBLE. I.E. PLACE IN A SAFETY DEPOSIT BOX, LOCKED IN A CAR TRUNK; OPERATOR DOES NOT HAVE THE KEY, SEVERAL OPERATORS GUARDING THE MONEY AND THE SUSPECT IS AWARE THAT THEY ARE THERE.

J. NEVER LET THE SUSPECT THINK THAT YOU CAN GET THE MONEY BACK BY SIMPLY MAKING A PHONE CALL.

5. DELIVERY OF THE DOPE.

A. REMEMBER IF YOU GET TOO HEAVY ON THE MONEY SHOW (WHEN YOU ARE IN THE DRIVER'S SEAT) THAT THE SUSPECT MIGHT DO THE SAME THING WHEN THE DOPE IS DELIVERED.

B. TRY TO SET THE DOPE DELIVERY SO THE COVERING TEAM WILL HAVE AN EASY CHANCE TO SEIZE IT.

C. PROVIDE CLUES OVER THE WIRE WHEN POSSIBLE— ROOM NUMBERS, LICENSE NUMBERS ETC.

6. ARREST.

A. SIGNAL—MAKE IT AN EASY WORD TO INCORPORATE INTO THE CONVERSATION AS YOU SEE THE DOPE. IE; THIS IS DYNAMITE DOPE. DYNAMITE BEING THE WORD.

B. USE THE SAME WORD EVERY TIME SO THAT EVERY-

ONE WILL KNOW EVEN IF IT IS OMITTED FROM THE GAME PLAN AND THE BRIEFING.

C. MONITORING OFFICER SHOULD NOT CALL THE ARREST, UNLESS THE SIGNAL IS GIVEN BY THE OPERATOR. EXCEPTION: SOMETHING THE OPERATOR IS NOT AWARE OF, (I.E., ARMED SUSPECTS ARRIVING IN THE AREA).

D. WHEN ARREST SIGNAL IS GIVEN, APPROACHING OFFICERS SHOULD RESPOND QUICKLY, WITHOUT NOISE AND WITH CAUTION; KEEP THE FOOT OUT OF THE CARB, IT CAN BE HEARD FOR BLOCKS, DO NOT SLAM CAR DOORS OR SQUEAL TIRES.

E. OPERATOR SHOULD NOT PARTICIPATE IN THE ARREST. ESPECIALLY CRITICAL IF NUMEROUS AGENCIES ARE INVOLVED IN THE ARREST. THE OPERATOR HAS DONE HIS JOB IN CONVINCING THE SUSPECTS THAT HE IS A CRIMINAL, ALL OF A SUDDEN HIS ROLE REVERSES AND HE ATTEMPTS TO MAKE AN ARREST. IF SHOT BY THE SUSPECTS, THEY WILL CLAIM SELF–DEFENSE, STATING THAT THEY THOUGHT THEY WERE ABOUT TO BE RIPPED OFF. THE OPERATOR MIGHT BE SHOT BY HIS OWN PEOPLE.

F. ALLOW THE OPERATOR TO WALK AWAY FROM THE SUSPECTS BEFORE COMING IN AND MAKING THE ARREST.

Chapter 7

INFORMANTS

It is well known that undercover cases are a result of some kind of involvement by an informant. As a matter of course, the outcome of a case will be greatly enhanced if the informant involved is well known or trusted by the suspects.

Many cases would be impossible to complete without having an informant's help. Informants are a necessary part of law enforcement and should be utilized to their fullest.

Before we get into the informant and his role I believe that there has to be an understanding of what is an informant, what is their motivation, how we can utilize informants and the pit falls of working with informants.

In law enforcement today we deal with three classifications of informants. One is the citizen informant, one is a tested informant and the last is an untested informant.

When we talk about a citizen informant we are referring to an individual, a citizen, who is in a position to provide information regarding some type of crime or criminal activity. This citizen is not involved in the criminal life and for the most part he is willing to assist law enforcement out of the goodness of his heart and civic pride. Because the citizen informant does not have anything to gain by supplying information to law enforcement, the requisites to show reliability of the information, which they supply, is less than that which is demanded of other informants.

The investigators have to be sure and state the difference between a citizen informant and any other type of informant.

A tested, reliable informant is usually someone who has been involved in some type of criminal activity and is able to supply information regarding that activity to law enforcement personnel. This type of inform-ant usually cooperates for one of the following reasons:

1) Money. This is the individual whom we affectionately refer to as a mercenary. Money makes the world go around and these informants like to get paid. They go out and work hard to put people in jail which in turn will create a cash flow for them. Keeping in mind that money is the

motivation behind these individuals we go in knowing that their loyalty is to the greenback. This individual will not hesitate to go shopping, looking for the highest bidder. He will call any law enforcement agency and ask them how much he could make by doing a case. He will continue calling agencies until he gets the highest bidder. As a matter of course I do not tell informants how much money they will make for a certain case. The Lieutenant and the Captain of the section, or other part of management, will decide what the payment will be. I only negotiate the amount. The payment will take place after the case is concluded. If law enforcement personnel would not tell informants how much they would get paid, prior to the culmination of the case, shopping would come to a halt. The amount of payment which will be received by the informant will be decided by numerous factors: the informant involvement in the case, the amount of narcotics or contraband seized, the quality of the suspect or suspects arrested and whether the informant will testify or not.

2) Consideration in a criminal case which is pending. This individual has been arrested and he does not want to go to jail. He will make a deal in order to stay out of prison. Whatever the arrangement, they will for the most part complete it. Sometimes, these individuals continue to work with law enforcement after their original arrangement has been completed. They then become paid informants.

On some cases the suspect who has been arrested will contact the officer who arrested him, through his attorney, wishing to work out a deal. After meeting and conferring with the District Attorney a deal is struck. The suspect is allowed to plead guilty and the sentencing is left open. His sentence will depend on what he does.

Two things to keep in mind. Do not get caught in the bigger cases. If you arrest somebody for 20 kilos who is a Columbian national, do not let him out of jail to work off a case. This guy will only spend enough time to get an airplane ticket and leave the country. The other thing to remember is not to let somebody out and simply let them do nothing for a long period of time. These people are using you. If the informant does not keep his word, talk to the District Attorney and have him put back in jail.

3) Revenge. This individual could be anyone. For instance a wife who has found out that her husband was cheating on her, or vice versa, a husband who has found out the same. A partner on a criminal enterprise who finds out his partner has stolen money or merchandize. Let the

imagination wander. Revenge can happen for almost anything. On revenge cases, the case agent has to move swiftly. There are many times when some individual gives information on a closely related individual. After that occurs the informant and the suspect make up. This will cause the information to stop and it is likely that the informant will then become an obstruction to the case.

4) The elimination of their competitors. This individual will enhance his criminal enterprise by turning in his competitors. At the same time he will learn law enforcement operations and the identity of officers with whom he meets regularly. All of this knowledge will be very important and highly productive while promoting illegal activity which he controls.

Do not forget the individual whom we call a "psycho." This guy will call the police and sound very credible regarding the information which he wishes to pass on. Once the officers go out and meet with this individual, it might not be very easy to detect that they are dealing with a "psycho." The officers will eventually be able to find out that the informant is not all together, but in the mean time they will have lost a lot of time.

The "psycho" calls many law enforcement agencies. He will continue this activity until he finds an individual who shows interest in his information. As stated before, these guys sound very credible at times. The information sounds great and they seemed to be legitimate. After we get through that, the true person comes out. The officer then runs away as fast as possible. Every agency should have a system where they can enter these "psychos." This system will save younger officers a lot of time when they come across these crazies.

Let us continue with the discussion of real informants.

In order for the informant to be held reliable, he must have supplied investigators with information in the past which has proven to be reliable. For the information to be reliable it must have led to seizures of contraband, the arrest of individuals or said information has proven true as it relates to criminal activity in the part of a suspect or suspects.

An untested informant is a tested informant without the proven track record. For instance the first time a case agent receives information from an informant, that informant is untested. He will become a tested informant once the information proves to be true and it results in seizures and or arrests. An untested informant could be someone who does not want to be known to the case agent and who has only called in the information, via the phone, into law enforcement personnel. The information of an untested informant becomes harder to use. The case agent has to corroborate the information in order to establish it reliably.

Many investigators have an ability to develop informants and to make them highly productive. In the process of working with these informants, the investigators lose sight of the fact that today's informant could very well be tomorrow's suspect.

It is because of this unknown and because of our loyalty to all of law enforcement, that we must not make our relationship with an informant a training session in the policies, procedures and tactics of law enforcement personnel. If the case agent of an operation discusses the way in which we, as law enforcement individuals, do business, the informant will be able to remember those procedures and tactics.

When the informant is involved in some sort of criminal activity, at a latter date, he will utilize the knowledge which he gained through the controlling agent. By utilizing that knowledge the informant, turned criminal, will avoid apprehension or, worse, he could jeopardize the safety of another law enforcement officer trying to operate him in an undercover capacity.

While it is necessary to involve the informant on a case, it is also necessary to try and make his involvement as short as possible. As soon as the undercover operator is confident of his ability to undertake the operation, the informant should begin his departure in the involvement of the case. The removal of the informant is not something that can be attained every time. This is only a goal and the more often we can reach that goal, the better.

There are cases where the involvement of the informant will be necessary throughout the whole case. For instance, there are locations into which an informant should be sent and an undercover officer should not. It would be counter productive to become specific about when to and when not to send an undercover officer into a situation. This again depends on the agency and the people involved in the operation. If a high degree of danger is possible, an informant could be the best individual to utilize.

As a supervisor, I understand that dealing with informants will result in the possibility of the case agent and the informant becoming closely related, resulting in the development of a personal relationship. By the mere fact that narcotics officers deal with informants daily, chances of this scenario occurring is great. However, as supervisors, we must not let that relationship develop. If it does it will become a detriment to the officer handling the informant and the agency for which we work. When dealing with informants, we have to maintain our objectivity and professionalism. Off duty contact with an informant shall not be permitted.

Each agency will activate policies regarding informants, their use and handling. I will state some safeguards which I have utilized in the past and have been useful in dealing with informants:

1) When a case agent meets with an informant he should be accompanied by one or more officers.

2) The squad supervisor shall meet all of the informants controlled by his subordinates.

3) When an informant is paid, the payment shall be witnessed by a second investigator, preferably a supervisor.

4) Regardless of the informant reliability, the information supplied by an informant should be corroborated.

5) The informant shall not be given the investigator's home address or home phone number.

Developing Informants

Developing informants is time consuming. The expertise developed, after working investigations for some time, will become an asset in informant development. One of the prerequisites that an investigator must have is to be honest. Don't tell an informant, that you are going to pay him a large amount of money or that you are going to keep him out of jail, if you can not come through. In other words don't write a check that you can not back.

Our first loyalty is to law enforcement. If you can help the informant without compromising yourself, your position and your agency, then go ahead and do the best you can.

I personally get calls by defense attorneys who know me and want to have their clients work off a case. I also receive numerous calls from other law enforcement officers who have informants but they are unable to use them. They refer the informants to me in order to work a specific case.

Being honest means using an informant from another agency for the time specified. There have been times when an informant has been recommended to me from another agency. The informant has turned out to be outstanding. After the case, I have sent the informant back, to the agent he came from, with no strings attached. This should be the norm in our business. There are some investigators who will try to recruit informants away from other law enforcement officers. Informants, regardless of how good they are, should not be played off between law enforcement officers.

The best way to recruit informants is through the interview process. After an individual has been arrested, he should be interviewed about the case in which he was involved and the possibility of working with law enforcement. As with any other type of interview, there are individuals who can get suspects to cooperate with them easily while there are others who could not get their mothers to talk to them. It is usually very productive to have an experienced investigator speak to a suspect. By the time that the interview is over, the investigator will have the suspect eating out of his hand. The suspect will be approachable and will probably cooperate.

The investigator, interviewing the suspect knows that the suspect is in dire need of help. After all, nobody wants to go to jail.

Another way to recruit informants is through the referral system. By referral I mean an informant who refers another informant or suspect to a case agent. As informants, these individuals continually associate with suspects who have been arrested and are out on bail. From talking to these suspects, the informants ascertain that they are looking for help and might want to cooperate. The informants then refer the suspects to their handling agents and the suspects become informants.

Protecting the Informant

Informants, just like anybody else, are concerned with their safety. This is due to the fact that they have to deal with and inform on suspects who would not hesitate to have them killed. It is because of this fact that law enforcement personnel have to take all of the steps necessary to maintain as confidential the identity of an informant.

Prior to undertaking an investigation, the investigator has to ascertain if the informant is agreeable in testifying or if he wishes to remain anonymous. Once the wishes of the informant are know, the investigator can proceed with the planning of the operation.

The wishes of the informant must be honored by the investigator. If it becomes known that the investigation cannot proceed without the informant being revealed, the investigator has a few choices at his disposal.

1) He could lie to the informant and proceed. This could cost the informant his life or at least it will cause that informant to never work with that investigator again. I do not recommend this approach. Be honest, tell the informant that without his testimony the case will not go forward. Give him a chance to decide.

2) The investigator can tell the informant that his involvement, if continued, will cause his identity to be known. The informant should be given an opportunity to get out of the investigation and the investigator should proceed to investigate the suspect by utilizing other means. The informant will get credit for the case; however, the payment he receives will be substantially less. This is due to the limited involvement.

3) The informant can remain in the case, culminating in the arrest of the suspect and the seizure of evidence. The informant will not be asked to testified or be disclosed. Since the testimony was necessary for the prosecution of the case, it will be likely that the case will be dismissed and the suspect will go free. It is also likely that the criminal case will not be filed before going to court. This will cause the earlier release of the suspect without further proceedings. Again this type of arrest will cause the payment to the informant to be diminished. This type of investigation is not the best way to proceed. While law enforcement gets the dope or contraband off the street, the suspect is free to continue with his criminal enterprise. It is up to the case agent, the supervisor and the district attorney to decide which way to approach the prosecution of the case.

In California it is easier to keep an informant confidential by prosecuting the case through the state courts. The District Attorneys, whom we deal with in Los Angeles County, are experts in the field and very helpful to law enforcement. It would be much more difficult to keep the informant confidential if the case is prosecuted through the federal courts. If the confidentiality of the informant is not a factor to consider, the federal system offers stiffer penalties and the proceedings are concluded more rapidly than in state courts.

Many individuals in law enforcement do not understand informants and are not at ease when utilizing them. For the most part these are individuals who have had a very limited experience, at best, in the use, cultivation, developing and use of informants.

If I were to make a point, which I felt was most important in the field of informants, it would be not to forget your loyalty to law enforcement and to act in a professional manner at all times. Never compromise your position.

I have had informants who have been outstanding and I have also had informants who were assisting me in order to promote their own criminal enterprises.

There was an informant who would always give me information on suspects who were dealing cocaine. I felt that the informant knew more than he was telling me. This guy would never give me enough information in order to complete the case. I always found myself having to do a lot of work in order to arrest a suspect and seize contraband. As this type of activity continued, I had a conversation with the informant. It was during this conversation that I found out why he was only giving me limited information. The informant was afraid that if he gave me too much information he would be known to the suspected target. Although I had told him that his identity would not be revealed, the informant felt that if it were necessary I would reveal him in order to complete the investigation. Even after that talk I was not able to convince him that I would keep him confidential. Eventually he left town.

On the other hand, I had an informant who would tell me everything. This informant was so good that within a one-year period she made a large amount of money in working with law enforcement. This inform- ant was and still is one of the best informants with whom I have ever been associated. If she said something was happening, it would occur as she had stated.

As it is with most women, this informant would hear things that no one else knew. She was able to tell me when, where and how much dope or money would be at a particular location. All I had to do was go and see the criminal activity take place. Informants like her can make law enforcement personnel look like outstanding investigators. She earned every penny she made.

As you can see, informants come in all shapes, colors and genders. They are an outstanding tool which will enhance law enforcement per- sonnel in their ability to apprehend suspects and seize contraband.

Regardless of how you feel about informants, they can be one of your best assets. If used properly they are worth their weight in gold.

Chapter 8

REVERSES

Reverses are quite new to the field of narcotics enforcement. A reverse investigation will be conducted by utilizing undercover methods. The complete investigation will be an undercover endeavor.

As usually happens with undercover operations, an informant will advise a case agent that someone is interested in purchasing an amount of narcotics. Because law enforcement will undertake the role of drug seller, there are many safety concerns and entrapment type issues that have to be addressed before the investigation proceeds.

From the start of the investigation to the ensuing operation, the undercover operator and the case agent have to become overly concerned with the likelihood of getting ripped off for the dope which they are about to sell.

The undercover operator has to define and continually access the way in which the investigation unfolds. The supervisor has to have the experience and the leadership capability necessary to set strongly defined parameters. The supervisor must also be able to terminate an investigation which displays the likelihood of a rip off or harm happening to his subordinates.

As with most undercover operations, the undercover operator is introduced to a suspect who wants to purchase the narcotics. The suspect, whom the undercover operator is meeting, will be involved in one of three things. He will in fact be interested in buying the narcotics. He could be looking to rip off a dope dealer (in this case the undercover operator is that dope dealer). Or, he is working with another law enforcement agency as an informant. In this last scenario we would have two law enforcement agencies working each other.

The best of these scenarios would be for the suspect to be a real dope dealer, in the market for some dope. The other two scenarios could become very complicated and very dangerous to all of the personnel involved.

If the suspect is in fact a dope dealer, looking for a new connection, the operation should continue. This operation must be handled with all of the care and concerns of any undercover operation. The personnel involved in this type of operation have to realize that the danger factor is quite high. The suspect has a strong feeling, rightfully so, that he is dealing with another criminal. It is quite easy for a narcotics dealer to injure or kill any associate involved in the illicit drug market.

The undercover operator has to keep the operation running smooth and safely. He has to do this without giving the buyer the impression that he will be an easy target for a rip off.

If successfully concluded, this type of operation will result in the seizure of the suspect's money. The suspect's arrest could also result in the possibility of being prosecuted for conspiracy to distribute narcotics.

One of the biggest obstacles faced during a reverse investigation is the issue of entrapment. Because of this I recommend, if possible, that the operator record all of the conversations with the suspect. The best evidence which we can present to a jury is photos of the suspects or recordings of the conversations during the negotiations. If at the time of prosecuting the case the District Attorney is armed with this type of evidence it will be likely that the entrapment issue will not be raised.

As a case against entrapment, the undercover operator has to be careful not to quote the suspect a price for the narcotics which is much lower than the going price in the open market.

Rip Off

If the suspected buyer has intentions of ripping off the undercover operator, only experience (on the part of the officers and the supervisor involved), and the mistakes made by the suspect will reveal those intentions.

The undercover operator, the case agent and the supervisor can take steps to undermine the suspect's ability to rip them off. During the planning of the operation the safety and control of the narcotics has to be of the utmost importance. The buyer cannot have prior warning as to where the dope is going to be or when he is going to see it. The dope has to be treated almost more restrictive than is money during a regular undercover operation.

This reasoning is simple to understand. When we deal with dope dealers and we are buying the dope, one of the first demands we encounter is for the undercover operator (the buyer) to show some money to the suspect. This demand is made by the suspect while stating that he wants to make sure that the operation is real. Another reason the suspect will have is that he does not want to move the dope before seeing the money. There are many reasons used by dope dealers. These suspects want to see the money before moving or displaying their wares.

The undercover operator, in a reverse investigation, has to make the same demands. Remember, the operator is taking the place of the dope dealer. Requesting to see money, before flashing dope, is the norm rather than the exception.

At this juncture in the negotiations our side has an advantage. If the operator is successful in having the suspect display the currency, the case can be terminated by seizing the money.

From a prosecution standpoint the case is not as strong as it could be. It would be a lot easier to prosecute the case if the suspect took possession of the dope and the undercover operator took possession of the money. That is from a prosecution stand point. In law enforcement our first priority is the safety of the officers involved in the operation. With that in mind, terminating the operation at the stage that the currency is shown will make it simpler for the supervisor to control the situation and safer for the officers involved.

If the District Attorney declines to criminally prosecute the suspect, we will seize the money and begin forfeiture proceedings.

Law enforcement strives for the conviction of suspects arrested while in the commission of a crime. With that in mind, we cannot let the guidelines set by the District Attorney dictate the way in which we handle safety and tactical matters. If we were to do that, decisions could be made that would jeopardize the safety of front line personnel. I would rather see a suspect walk free, than to sacrifice the life of a law enforcement officer in order to get a conviction.

There is a big chance that a reverse operation will not be completed if the suspects are planning a rip off. If the operation is planned properly the suspect will not get the chance to attempt the rip off of the operator. The suspect will tell the undercover operator that too many demands are being made—demands which he can not meet. This will cause the termination of the deal by the suspect.

The operator, case agent and the supervisor cannot make unsafe changes in the plans simply because the suspect begins to back out of the deal. If a deal is terminated by the suspect for no apparent reason, the likelihood that the deal was a rip off is high. Let's face it, when an undercover deal hangs up we never know the real reason. Look at a deal which has hung up and think positively. A reverse which is hung by a suspect has to be categorized as a success. Although no seizures or arrests were made, all of the officers involved went home safely.

One of the newest challenges which we face, in undercover operations, is the situation where suspects identify themselves as police officers in an attempt to rip off drug dealers of their money and narcotics. This type of rip off could be very dangerous. If the undercover operator or the covering team are not able to immediately identify the suspects as police impersonators, the wait that will take place in order to verify the identity of the suspects will cause problems during the attempted arrest. It is because of this that good communications and working relations, between neighboring law enforcement agencies, is very important.

It is my hope that investigators involved in undercover operations do not go back to the office, at the conclusion of an unsuccessful case, and begin to tell the undercover operator that the deal would have been consummated had he made the changes that the suspect requested. This type of attitude promotes disaster within a unit and the undercover operator cannot give in to the suspect's demands in order to successfully complete a given case.

Informants

The third and last scenario would be for the suspected buyer to be an informant. The first time that the suspect/informant meets the undercover operator, it is possible that the suspect/informant would be alone. Because he is alone the surveillance units, covering the undercover operator, are not able to detect other surveillance units in the area.

If the suspect is an informant, it will be easy to detect surveilling units from another agency at one of the meets during the negotiations. These units will be present in order to cover the informant and to identify the suspect, who in this case is the undercover operator.

Some areas in the country have checking systems that law enforcement personnel can query in order to see if an investigation is being worked by two agencies simultaneously. If this is not the case, in the area which your agency operates, the case agent has to go out of his way to identify the suspect who is meeting with the undercover operator. The case agent has to also contact all of the neighboring law enforcement agencies, including federal agencies, in his area.

After all of the checks have been completed the case agent, the supervisor and the surveilling units have to maintain a very alert posture. They will not only be looking for possible suspects, they will be also looking for possible law enforcement personnel.

During the arrest portion of a reverse investigation, it will be overly important that all of the arresting officers involved wear their identifying vests and jackets. By doing this it will give other law enforcement officers—if in fact another agency is involved and has not been detected until the arrest—the chance to stop before engaging in a deadly confrontation.

As long as we undertake reverse type operations there is a great chance for law enforcement personnel to get involved in working against each other, with each agency thinking that the individual whom they are meeting is a suspect. Because of this, it is important to promote good communication and working relations among all of the law enforcement agencies throughout the country.

Undercover operations are very dangerous and we have to extract the chance of having law enforcement officers harm each other due to miscommunications and improper identification.

Chapter 9

ISSUES OF IMPORTANCE

The following issues are most important to the field of narcotics enforcement and are addressed in the hope that the professionalism in this field is continued and expanded.

Testifying

Once the investigation concludes, with the arrest of a suspect or suspects, the judicial proceedings will begin. Law enforcement will have ended their involvement in the investigation. The District Attorney will continue with the prosecution of the suspects.

While law enforcement will still play a major part in the suspect's prosecution, it is the responsibility of the prosecutor to take the case to its conclusion.

The undercover officer in the case will carry the burden of doing most of the testifying in the case. Many things will take place during the defense phase of a trial involving an undercover operation.

There is a myth that if an undercover case results in a prosecution, the District Attorney will acquire a guilty verdict easily. The undercover officer has negotiated with a suspect to buy an amount of narcotics or, in the case of a reverse, to sell an amount of narcotics. At the end of the case the suspect is arrested and the officers involved in the case recover an amount of narcotics, money or both. The prevailing feeling is that this type of case would be an open and shut case, right? Wrong.

Real life and the prosecution of a case, such as the one described above, are not that simple. The entrapment defense will raise its ugly head. By the time the defense attorney gets through with the undercover officer, during cross examination, he will have the officer identified as the biggest narcotics trafficker in the world. The same attorney will portray his client as a poor soul who was misguided into selling some dope so that he could afford to make a large donation to the Mother Theresa Orphanage.

It is because of these types of maneuvers by defense attorneys and because juries are not aware of reality, as it applies to dope deals and undercover operations, that law enforcement personnel must continue to excel and be committed to professionalism during the prosecution phase of the case.

The supervisor, the case agent and the undercover operator can take certain steps, prior to the arrest, which will make the prosecution of the case easier to undertake by the District Attorney. These steps will go a long way in stopping any charges of entrapment being leveled by the defense.

If the undercover officer is a good looking female, it is most important that she does not wear revealing clothing or any enticing type of clothing that could be misconstrued as bait. After all, even if the female operator has conducted herself professionally throughout the investigation, it is possible that the defense attorney will claim that his client did the dope deal in order to impress the female operator. This, the defense counsel will tell the jury, was done by his client in order to gain sexual favors with her. If on top of that, the defense attorney can show that the female operator wore revealing clothing those problems could be compounded and the jury will begin to believe the charges being made.

The undercover operator cannot make promises to the suspect which could be construed as enticing. Promises such as, "We can go out on a date after the deal is over," or "I like you but, I will not mix business and pleasure. Let's finish the deal and we can then go out," will be easily attacked by the defense and will more than likely cause concern in the eyes of the jury.

This type of defense does not only apply to female operators. Male operators are also included. This is true if the suspect with whom they are dealing happens to be a female.

One of the pluses that an undercover officer has is the ability to keep good notes and a chronological report of all of the meetings and negotiations which take place up to the arrest. These notes will be incorporated into the arrest report, or, as an additional report, to be used by the prosecutor during court proceedings. These notes will also be very helpful as the undercover operator refreshes his memory months after the suspect's arrest.

Another factor which the defense attorney will point out, during an entrapment defense, will be the price which the undercover operator was willing to pay for the narcotics which he was to buy from the suspect. If the suspect's prices are way out of the normal range, of the going price at the time, the defense attorney could claim that the operator agreed to purchase the dope at a high price, causing the suspect into doing what he would not otherwise have done. Hence the poor soul was entrapped into being a dope dealer!

Depending on the various agency regulations and procedures, it would be very productive to record the conversations of all the meets which take place between the undercover operator and the suspect. While it would be very helpful to do so, it has to be understood that sometimes the cost to record all of the conversations becomes prohibitive. The supervisor has to decide whether the investigation warrants the recording of the meets and all other conversations.

The undercover operator wears the wire for safety reasons. The wire is not an instrument which should be looked at as a tool to make the prosecution of the suspects easier. If by wearing the wire the prosecution becomes easier to undertake, due to the recordings of the meet etc., then that becomes a plus.

When an undercover operator appears in the courtroom, to testify in front of a jury, his demeanor and professionalism become of the utmost importance. The undercover operator will state the facts in answering questions from both the prosecution and the defense. He is there to testify as to what occurred. The operator cannot show partiality towards the prosecution or the defense. His job is to relay what he experienced, to the jury. The jury will decide on the guilt or innocence of the suspect being tried.

Preparation, before testifying, becomes exceedingly important. If an officer appears in court without the proper preparation, he will certainly become a poor witness and the defense attorney will have a field day.

As a young narcotics officer I was involved in a case which was about to go to a jury trial. Prior to appearing in court I glanced through the reports and did not prepare myself as well as I should have. I felt at the time that I was well versed in everything that would take place.

On the day that I was to testify, I encountered a defense attorney who had prepared himself thoroughly. He went over all of the questions in the preliminary hearing. At the time that I was crossexamined the defense attorney asked me a question and I gave him the answer I thought was proper. As it turned out I had answered the same question differently in the preliminary hearing. As I finished answering the question, I remembered the discrepancy. I brought it to the attention of the defense counsel. I went on to answer the question, correcting myself, as I had during the preliminary hearing.

Even after changing the answer it took some time for me to explain to the jury my inability to answer the question the same way as I had done previously. As a matter of fact, the defense attorney used my contradictory answers as one of the main points to attack my credibility. His attacks on my credibility and my memory retention continued for as long as I continued to testify.

This attorney utilized my answers in order to attack me during the closing arguments in the trial. I was portrayed as incompetent, forgetful and possibly a liar.

As it turned out the jury believed me and found the suspect guilty. Nevertheless, I should have prepared myself better. Had I done that, the trial which lasted two days would have surely been shorter. It was obvious that the defense attorney did not have any other points to attack during the defense portion of the trial. I could have lost the case for the prosecution.

Training

This is one area where all of the agencies, involved in the field of narcotics enforcement, fall short of the needs of their officers.

All agencies put their officers/agents through a recruit academy which lasts anywhere from 3 to 6 months in length. In this academy the officers learn procedures, law, the policies of the agency, self defense and an assorted number of different subjects. Mixed in with all of these subjects the officers receive a minimal amount of narcotics training. (All this applies to the academy of all agencies except DEA where the emphasis is on narcotics enforcement. That enforcement is their primary objective.)

At the conclusion of their training the new officers/agents are assigned to the field. Those in local law enforcement begin their regular patrol duties and will continue in that assignment for a few years before going on to an assignment in the field of investigations.

The federal agents get assigned to a field office and begin a new phase of training. For all law enforcement officers the new training involves hands-on and on the job training. This type of training is the bulk of the training which will be received by these officers/agents.

After spending some years on the job, the local officers have the opportunity to be assigned to a narcotics enforcement detail. After being assigned to the field of narcotics enforcement these officers receive most of their training on the job. In the Los Angeles Police Department we put our officers through a two-week narcotics school. They learn basic narcotics subjects and procedures. They then become narcotics officers. They will be assigned to work with more experienced officers.

Most agencies are involved in the field of narcotics enforcement, in one way or another, regardless of what their primary objective is. The officers/agents who are assigned to the field of narcotics enforcement receive the majority of their training on the job, with experienced officers training the younger officers.

Many narcotic officers attend seminars and classes which are put on by organizations such as The California Narcotics Officers Association. These associations present monthly training for the narcotics officers.

The individual departments attempt to put on training days having to do with narcotics enforcement. I have attended such training days only to be exposed to classes having to do with earth quake preparedness and hepatitis B instead of narcotics training.

What I see as the real problem is the inability of the different agencies/departments to provide proper training for their officers/agents.

Training is a costly endeavor. A properly trained officer will not make stupid mistakes while in the discharge of his duties. While teaching the Undercover Officer Survival Class, I have been exposed to many seasoned narcotics officers/agents who are still operating years behind the times. Their tactics, planning and execution of operations lack the proper and safe methods by which they will survive. Because of poor training, these officers/agents have not been exposed to new procedures and tactics which they can utilize as they attempt to reach their daily objectives.

We in the narcotics enforcement community have to do better in putting forth regular training and exchanging of ideas. This should be done so that young, inexperienced officers will have a chance to learn the proper procedures and to maintain a safe environment in which to work.

I will not hesitate, when requested to do so, to appear at other agencies and departments in order to make a presentation, having to do with undercover officer survival. If our agencies/departments do not give us the proper training, it is incumbent upon us to do the best job possible to train those officers working under our command.

Term Limits

Detectives involved in the field of narcotics enforcement become experienced and are able to utilize that experience during the discharge of their duties. In order to gain this experience these officer/detectives have to spend between one and three years as front-line officers. It is because of this that I want to address the time limit which is placed on specialized assignments by some agencies.

As I travel around the country, teaching the undercover survival class, I am astonished at the number of departments that place a time limit on detectives/officers assigned to the field of narcotics enforcement.

During the classes and seminars, I would speak to numerous staff officers from different departments. Through these conversations, I was able to ascertain that there were as many reasons, for the time limits, as there were departments involved. I will go over some of the most prevalent reasons:

1.) Many of the staff officers would point out that by rotating officers out of narcotics assignments they could avert corruptive practices by those officers. Another view which the staff officers would use, would be the fact that by rotating the officers out of the narcotics assignment they were able to rotate new officers into the field. This they felt gave the new officers a break from their daily routines and exposed them to a new experience.

2.) The staff officers felt that those officers who were leaving the narcotics assignment would be able to utilize their newly acquired expertise in their new department functions.

3.) The last factor which these staff officers would point out was the fact that narcotics officers would become overly comfortable in the field of narcotics enforcement. After spending time in this field these officers would not attempt to be promoted to higher ranks within the structure of their agency.

After listening to all of the various opinions and having personally observed this field for years, I would like to respond. I do this in the hopes that the term limit movement is reversed or amended. I had felt quite comfortable with the staff officers of my own department on this point. I had always been told that our staff officers understood the need for experience in this field. With this understanding, the issue of term limits was not a hot topic within my agency. This only lasted until recently when I listened to an Assistant Chief from the L.A.P.D., the same Assistant Chief who has command control over narcotics, who stated that it was his belief that narcotics detectives could best serve the department by being placed on a rotating basis in and out of the narcotics group.

The first point which I will address will be the stopping of corruption by rotating officers. A few years ago I was assigned to a task force of the L.A.P.D. and the L.A.S.O. The sergeant in charge of the squad prior to my arrival, Sergeant Sobel, had left to head a new squad assigned to work major violator cases. Because of his transfer I was asked to go to the unit along with a sergeant from L.A.S.O. as the new supervisors.

From the time that I got to the new assignment I was able to ascertain that the unit was not operating in the mode under which the officers from the L.A.P.D. were accustomed to operate. It was my belief that the policies which we were working under (those were the L.A.S.O. policies) made for much to lose. It was my personal feeling, at the time, that if the L.A.P.D. was to stay within the structure of the task force it was likely that I would not be able to control all of the actions of the officers under my supervision.

I approached my commanding officer and asked him to remove the L.A.P.D. squad from the task force. I told him that if we stayed in that setting the policies which were being utilized would cause disruption in the ability of our officers to follow L.A.P.D. rules and regulations. Furthermore, I advised my commanding officer that these rules lent themselves to corruptive practices.

Here I was, a low line supervisor telling our command structure the shortcomings of another department—a department, which by the way, is one of the best in the nation.

Our command took my recommendation and decided to break up the task force.

While all of this was happening, and without my knowledge, the L.A.S.O., the L.A.P.D. and the F.B.I. were conducting an investigation into the corruptive practices of members of the task force. The investigation covered the period prior to my arrival.

Sergeant Sobel was the main witness in the federal case. Although he was the leader of the corruptive practices, Sobel would testify against his subordinates and peers.

If, in fact, corruption took place within the task force, I say "if, in fact," because I did not have personal knowledge of these practices, (it must be pointed out that numerous deputies were convicted during the ensuing trial); being a believer of the judicial system, I have to say that corruption was running rampant and the evidence proved that conjecture. It is my belief that the corruption took place because of the lax practices, department procedures and poor supervision.

The officers involved in these practices would have engaged in corruption had they been working another assignment and had they been given the same opportunities. There were many other narcotics detectives who did not engage in such practices.

Because of all the media attention, the Sheriffs Department initiated a rotation basis by which the deputies, assigned to narcotics enforcement, would work.

In other words the Sheriff threw out the baby with the bath water. Had upper management done their job properly, it would have been very unlikely that the corruption, which was uncovered, would have involved such a large number of officers. Rotating officers in and out of the specialized assignment is more of a political expedient statement than a cure to avert future corruptive practices.

We in law enforcement recruit our people from the society at large. To my knowledge there is no way that the process will expose all of the bad apples applying to be police officers. Management has to prepare themselves in order to expose and stop these bad apples which end up embarrassing and corrupting other officers. If management places the right policies and safeguards in place, along with the proper audits, these occurrences would be minimal.

Certainly, rotating officers will not stop corruption from taking place. As a matter of fact, if the officers going into a narcotics assignment are aware of the short duration, they will not be as dedicated as they should be towards the job and the section for which they will work.

The second point is the rotating of officers out of a specialized assignment in order to give other officers a break from their daily duties. This practice is counter productive. If an officer needs a break, from his daily duties, it would be much cheaper for the agency by which he is employed to send him on an extended vacation rather than give him an assignment to a specialized field like narcotics enforcement.

If the rotation takes place every three years, the officer going into the assignment knows he has three years before he goes back to a patrol assignment. This will cause him not to put his whole soul into the job. The officer knows that once he leaves narcotics he will return to a uniform job and the time spent in narcotics would only be a breather.

After returning to patrol, his knowledge in the field of narcotics will diminish with time. It will be impossible for the patrol officer to stay updated in all of the new case law and procedures in the field of narcotics enforcement. The officer will spend much of his time answering radio calls, which for the most part have nothing to do with narcotics enforcement.

Another draw back to rotating officers would be the loss of experience to the unit. At no time, will there be any officer with more than three years of experience assigned to the unit. This will cause safety concerns for the young officers, since there will not be anyone in the section who has the experience to stop a poorly run operation. Three years is not enough time, experience wise, even in a uniform assignment. I remember, as a young patrol officer, a sergeant telling me that I would not be worth anything to the department until I had had five years of experience working uniform.

With a minor adjustment some of these agencies could have both the experience and the rotation that they want. Let's say that the agency has a narcotics enforcement unit which has six officers and one supervisor. I would recommend that the supervisor and at least three of the officers remain as permanent members of the squad. The other three openings could be rotated as recommended by the agency. By doing the rotation in this fashion the department would not be at a loss for experience during tactical operations.

There is a factor that some of these agencies neglect to address. That is the liability which will be encountered by a municipality due to the inexperience of a supervisor or senior officer running any operation.

If an officer were killed, due to the inexperience caused by the rotating policy, and it could be shown that by having a more experienced supervisor the officer's life could have been saved, it is my belief that the municipality will be liable for their inability to provide a safe environment for its employees to work.

A time limit of two to three years gives the officers assigned to that unit the needed background with which to become somewhat proficient. Most narcotics officers take longer than that to become experts in their fields. To move them at that time would be costly to the agency and a waste of personnel.

When someone in command states that a seasoned narcotics officer can utilize his expertise in either the patrol field or any other detective function, I can safely say that the person making that statement does not have the narcotics background with which to base his opinion.

If tomorrow I were to be assigned to work a homicide section while a homicide supervisor was to assume my duties, I could safely state that neither one of us would be able to be productive for a long period of time. I would be unable to tell the difference between a dead body and a mannequin. The homicide detective would not be able to supervise an operation and to distinguish between a safe operation and an operation heading for disaster. This inexperience could cost the life of an officer, an informant or a civilian in the area where the operation is taking place.

I have been in the field of narcotics for most of my law enforcement career. While I commend those within my agency who are trying to promote and better themselves, personally, I'm very happy with my rank and assignment. I do not need someone from a staff position telling me that I would do much better if I were promoted within the agency structure. If I wanted to promote, to a higher rank, I would take the necessary steps to assure my promotability. Promotions should be left up to the individual officers.

The bottom line, in the rotation of the officers in and out of specialized assignment, is the loss of experience, and by that loss the agency will lose the time it spent in the training and development of those officers.

In rotation, both the officer and the agency lose. The officer's morale is not as good as it would be if he were assigned to an assignment of his choice. An officer will not be as productive, knowing that the assignment is of short duration.

Specialized units should be an assignment which will be occupied by those officers who have shown the ability and willingness to sacrifice themselves in order to attain excellence. Not everyone should work a specialized unit nor should the assignment be made a reward given to officers who need a break from patrol.

If management wants to eradicate corruption they should conduct financial investigations of all officers assigned to the field of narcotics enforcement. The internal affairs section should also conduct regular sting type operations on these officers.

There is no substitute for experience. This experience is the difference between life and death. If we take the experience factor out of the daily narcotics operations it will be likely that more narcotics officers will be killed or injured in the discharge of their daily duties.

Survival is a daily objective and experience is the best guarantee to staying alive.

Exposure to the Media

It seems as if law enforcement has been utilized as an avenue for the creation of numerous so called cop shows on TV. While most agencies do and should cooperate with the media and many of those shows, there are instances where I believe we expose too much of the secrets and procedures by which we operate on a daily basis.

We have to keep in mind that television is driven by ratings. The different networks will not produce a show that does not draw the viewing audience. In order for the networks to draw the audience they have to produce a weekly show which will give the audience as much of the action, blood and guts as can be televised. I personally do not agree with that premise but, if that is what people want to watch, so be it.

My concerns arise when I watch a show on TV and I see some narcotics officer explaining to the whole world how we, in the narcotics enforcement field, operate and how we undertake our operations.

There is one show, in particular, which I have seen off and on. I watch this show rarely since I get quite sick when I watch it. The host of this show was or is the officer in charge of a small narcotics unit in the Northwest. This guy has done more to expose the way in which undercover and narcotics operations are undertaken than anyone else I have come across. If you were to watch this show you could see how undercover or narcotics operations are planned and executed, how the money is marked before we buy dope, which type of listening device undercover officers carry and many of the little secrets which we use when approaching houses to serve a search warrant or arrest the suspects.

Of course, this so called narcotics supervisor is doing all this in his quest to gain ratings. I am not against cooperating with the media, but there is a fine line that we cannot cross. We in law enforcement do not have a lot of tools that we can utilize in order to stay ahead of the suspects whom we are trying to apprehend. As a matter of fact those suspects are better armed and better equipped than we are. It is because of this that we cannot let the whole world see everything that we do and how we do it.

Not only does this show expose all the secrets and procedures which we utilize, what I find most disgusting is the fact that this show host/dope supervisor, exposes the identity of undercover officers and informants. This could become dangerous for those individuals. It seems as if the operations are planned with the show in mind, rather than having the filming depict the operation as it unfolds.

Again, while I am not an advocate of shutting the media out of our operations, I would like to see a little more restraint in the exposure of these operations, our policies and equipment.

Keep this in mind. You could be operating in some town in the Midwest. The equipment which you utilize and expose, on television, is the same equipment which is used all over the nation. The exposure of that equipment or the exposure of a sensitive procedure could end up costing the life of a brother undercover operator somewhere else.

Everyone wants to be a movie star. Next time you get a chance to have the television cameras rolling, think of those officers who daily risk their lives in the field of narcotics enforcement. Give those cameras as much as they need without compromising the safety of your brother officers.

Task Forces

Due to many reasons, i.e. pooling of resources, money savings, larger units, etc., the field of narcotics enforcement is rapidly moving towards the task force mode. It is my belief that task forces are an outstanding use of personnel, especially now that the cities and counties find themselves strapped for money to fund such specialized fields. Members from all of the departments working together, will form a close friendship and working relationship. The departments would be able to draw officers from a larger pool of manpower. The newly found relationship between these officers will continue even after they complete their assignment and return to other jobs in their respective departments.

One of the larger obstacles in a task force is the different policies and procedures of all the departments involved. As I stated in a previous chapter, it is important for the supervising officer, of an integrated squad, to understand all of the various policies and procedures that all of the different officers work under.

I have found the best way to handle all of these policies is for the supervisor to adhere to the most conservative and restricted policies. By doing this, the supervisor would never violate the policy of the officers from the more liberal departments.

While there are many benefits to task forces, there are also some drawbacks. One of these drawbacks is the fact that some departments involved do not send the best individuals they have. These departments end up sending inexperienced officers who have to be trained by the more experienced officers.

Many departments would rather have their best people assigned to their own department. The thinking is, that if a local unit seizes an amount of money, the department and municipality for which they work will receive the bulk of that money.

The fact still remains that an assignment to a task force will result in the enhancement of individual officers and their exposure to different methods and experiences which will make those officers better and more productive upon their return to their respective agencies.

It is my belief that task forces are the thing of the future and they will expand.

Chapter 10

DIFFERENT LEVELS

Street Operations

For the last few years sales of drugs, by street dealers, have risen considerably. This phenomenon initiated what is commonly referred to as the drive-up system of drug dealing.

The suspects involved in street sales stand in plain view at a corner or sidewalk, in a residential or business neighborhood. These suspects will openly solicit individuals, driving or walking by the area. This is done in order to let the buyer know of their presence and for advertising purposes.

These individuals can be independent drug dealers. They could be associated with a criminal organization or employed by a local gang. Because of the competition and the involvement of gangs, the likelihood for violence is great.

The citizens who frequent, live and work in the area where street dealers operate, have become alarmed due to the propensity for violence by these suspects. They also have a concern because of the criminal atmosphere created by the element which is drawn to this kind of activity.

One of the tools utilized to combat this problem is the use of undercover officers. These officers are sent to a targeted area in order to buy drugs from the street dealers. After the operators make their buys, the arrest team places the suspects into custody.

Officers assigned to these operations are, for the most part, young. Their appearance can be as varied as the scenario dictates. Street dealers deal with individuals ranging from addicts to business people.

The undercover operator and the arrest team, in a street buy setting, can be compared to soldiers involved in guerilla warfare. The operator is sent into a hot area, his mission being to single out and buy drugs from the street dealers. Once the deal is completed, the arrest team is sent into the buy location where they locate and arrest the suspect.

Because of the many locations where street deals take place, the operator, his supervisor and the arrest team will go into different areas within the city. This group of officers will try to stop the blatant sales of drugs by these suspects.

For the most part street buy-bust operations are short in duration and productive. The danger which these operators face is very high. Street dealers are involved in robberies of their clients and they sell what is referred to as bunk dope (bunk dope is an item that looks like the drugs that the client is attempting to buy, but it is not drugs). These young operators are under tremendous pressure while making the drug buys.

The operators must be alert, be able to retain information and suspect description, as well as keeping their safety in mind. These operators are asked to make multiple buys during their work day. These buys will be made from different suspects, at different locations. Because of this, their retention ability is important. This ability will assist the operator in the completion of the reports, the booking of evidence and eventually his testimony at the court proceedings.

All of the safeguards and concerns, which I have discussed previously, come into play in these operations. Undercover officer survival will still be the most important item in everyone's mind. The only difference, between street buying and a major deal, is the amount of drugs or other contraband being purchased and the frequency of the buys undertaken by each undercover operator.

The arrest team, in a street buy-bust operation, also faces tremendous danger. These officers engage in daily foot pursuits and altercations. The suspects protect their turf and will not hesitate to ambush the arresting officers.

Street dealers have a higher propensity for violence than other drug dealers. Very often these dealers are addicts and ex-cons who have nothing to lose. These suspects will arm themselves to protect their wares and they will be more likely to get involved in a deadly confrontation with the police or their competitors than other dealers.

Mid Level/Major Violators

The operators involved in this category are very experienced and talented. As I have stated before, buying dope is an art and these guys are the top of the line in their craft.

These operators become involved in operations that will take any- where from one day to a few weeks to complete. For the most part these operators do not engage in long term relationships with the suspects whom they are trying to operate.

Operators in the Mid Level/Major Violator operations will attempt to purchase an amount of drugs, ranging from one kilo to numerous kilos. If he is successful, the operation will conclude with the arrest of the suspect at the time that the drugs are delivered.

On rare occasions, the operator is allowed to buy-walk an amount of drugs. Buy walk, meaning that the operator buys an amount of drugs and the suspect is not immediately arrested. This allows the operator to order an amount larger than the amount which he purchased originally. The reason for the first buy would be to enhance the credibility of the operator in the eyes of the suspect.

Again, I want to emphasize, there cannot be any deviation from the officer survival procedures which have already been outlined. Any drug buy or the buy of any contraband, regardless of the amount, is a dangerous undertaking.

While the amounts may differ between street and Mid Level/Major Violators, their mission is the same. The danger which they face is also the same.

Long-Term Assignment

The long-term assignment is unlike anything previously discussed in this book. For the most part, all of the safeguards and procedures previously outlined do not apply in this area of undercover operations.

Operators assigned to this type of investigations include local officers and State and Federal agents. Long term operations can take years to complete.

The operator assigned to this perilous assignment, is faced with physical as well as great psychological risk. The psychological problems, faced by these operators, become quite obvious after the termination of the assignment.

Long term assignments will require the infiltration of the operator into a criminal organization. Infiltrating a criminal enterprise is a time consuming task. The operator will spend long periods of time with the criminal element, while at the same time cutting off his ties with law enforcement peers, his friends and sometimes family members.

Assumption of a criminal personality, by the operator, is the norm.

His partners and peers are not able to cover the operator as he goes about his daily duties. The operator is on his own.

The assignment becomes a way of life. This would be the beginning of the psychological problems.

As an officer in the early 70's I was asked to be part of two, long-term, undercover operations. On one occasion I declined. The second time I accepted the challenge. The operation which I agreed to undertake was shorter, in duration, than originally thought.

From this limited experience, I began to realize the dangers in these long-term operations and the stress which is placed on the operator, his family and friends.

The first assignment I was offered was a job in the now defunct Public Disorder Intelligence Division. This division was involved in intelligence gathering as it pertained to subversive groups. This assignment would require me to infiltrate a hispanic group known as "The Venceremos Brigade." The nucleus of this group was comprised of college age individuals. They were militant in nature and communist in their political affiliation. I was interested in the assignment. This interest diminished when I was told that it was certain that I would have to travel to Cuba once I joined the group. This travel would be necessary as part of the group's indoctrination and training.

Travel to Cuba was disguised, by members of this group, as an attempt to help the Cuban government with the sugar harvest. In reality, the group went to Cuba in order to receive training on bomb construction and the setting of bomb devices. The members would also be instructed in civil disobedience and other revolutionary methods.

The assignment itself was not a problem. Travelling to Cuba was. I had left Cuba as a small child and was not about to return under the communist regime. Needless to say I declined the offer.

The next assignment had to do with infiltrating a Cuban gambling organization. This organization was based in Los Angeles with connections in New York and Miami. The organization would take bets through the Puerto Rican and Mexican lotteries.

In order to infiltrate the organization, I was severed of all law enforcement ties and affiliations. I was given a residence in the city and was requested to spend most of my time in my new lifestyle and with the suspects associated with the criminal enterprise.

At the time, I was married and had two daughters. My absence created hardships for my family and the stress level was quite high.

The assignment lasted a few months and was successfully completed. Even in that short amount of time I could experience the dangers, both physical and psychological, in that type of operation.

An operator who is asked to infiltrate organized crime or a drug organization, will be exposed to a lifestyle to which he is not accustomed. The operator, who has for most of his life been a law abiding individual, is asked to become a criminal, associate with criminals and become a successful criminal.

The mental and personality changes that take place are drastic. If the operator remains in that assignment for one, two or three years, he forgets his previous loyalties and begins to identify with the life which he is leading.

Many of these long-term operators cannot shed their criminal personalities after the completion of their assignment. They will continue to operate outside the law. Sometimes, drinking becomes a problem and many times these operators are arrested, ending their law enforcement careers. All of these things occur as a result of the assignment and the operator not being able to adjust to his old environment, once the investigation is over.

I have no answers to correct the problems which are faced by long-term operators. The agencies involved, in these types of operations, have to continually assess the danger to their officers versus the need for these types of operations to take place.

Long-term undercover operations are a needed element in law enforcement. The officers who volunteer to undertake these assignments should receive some type of psychological backing and training. The agencies should maintain contact with them. This contact is necessary in order to reinforce the operator's loyalty to law enforcement.

Once the assignment terminates, the agency should implement a program where the operator is psychologically debriefed and deprogrammed. There must be some sort of support system in place for the operator and his family.

Many operators spend years in undercover assignments. One day they are driving expensive vehicles, eating in fancy restaurants, wearing expensive clothing and jewelry and are involved in a criminal life. The following day they are asked to drive a four year old Plymouth, eat fast food and work within a regimented environment. That is quite a shock.

As I have stated before, I have no answer to these problems. It is incumbent upon the agencies to come up with guidelines and procedures which will address this problem.

No operation should be placed above the well being of a law enforcement officer.

Informants could be an option that can be utilized on these operations. Even though they would be very difficult to control, the risk to sworn personnel would diminish.

Long-term operations will continue to take place. The operators in these operations should be closely screened, monitored and supported. If the operator shows any type of personality or psychological change, the operation should be terminated and the operator should be returned to his regular assignment.

Chapter 11

UNDERCOVER CASES

We will analyze numerous undercover narcotics operations. These operations resulted in the death or injury of the undercover operators. These cases will be discussed in order to promote dialogue between the personnel within a unit and in order to point out those mistakes which caused the problems. These cases are not used as a means of putting any particular individual or agency down. As a matter of fact, I will not mention the names of the agencies involved.

Keep in mind that all of the officers involved in these cases were hard working officers. This could happen to any of you. The only difference between these officers and those of you involved in the field of narcotics enforcement, presently, is the different training you receive, the geographics and the fact that these officers cannot change what has already happened. YOU CAN!

Marty

Marty was an undercover officer from a local police department in the northeast part of the country. He was assigned to a task force made up of local and federal officers. His best friend, a sergeant by the name of Gary, was also assigned to the task force.

Marty had made three undercover buys of 1/8 ounce of heroin from a suspect. Marty had made each buy inside the suspect's residence.

The residence was a three story house. On the first floor there was a candy store. Living quarters were located on the second and third floors of the residence. The suspect conducted all of the sales on the third floor.

During a conversation between Marty and the suspect, the suspect bragged to Marty that he had killed an individual and had not been arrested for the crime. After the conversation Marty left the location and went to the State Attorney's office to discuss the possible homicide. The State Attorney verified that there was an unsolved homicide that fit the description of the crime described by the suspect. The State Attorney asked Marty to return to the suspect's residence, while wearing a small tape recorder, in order to engage the suspect in conversation regarding the homicide. The State Attorney wanted to record incriminating statements by the suspect while they discussed the homicide.

Marty agreed and the task force set up to cover him. They were in possession of arrest/search warrants for the suspect and his residence.

Marty went into the suspect's residence and began to talk to the suspect. The conversation continued for some time and Marty felt that it was time for him to exit the residence in order to change the tape in the recorder. Marty had not been successful in having the suspect talk about the homicide up to that point. Marty told the suspect that he wanted to go out and buy some cigarettes. Marty left and went to meet with Gary and the rest of the crew.

Gary and Marty met and a new tape was placed into the recorder. Marty told Gary that the suspect was walking inside the house with a .357 magnum revolver in his waist band. Gary told Marty that he should not go back inside. Gary told Marty that they already had the warrant for the suspect and the house. The suspect was armed and he would feel better if Marty remained outside while the covering team served the warrant.

Marty convinced Gary that everything would be OK, that he would go back inside in an attempt to get the suspect to talk about the homicide. Gary told Marty that the covering team would wait until he, Marty, either came out with the suspect in custody or until he came out alone.

Time passed and Gary had no communication with Marty. Gary called the office and had a phone call placed into the suspect's house. Gary told the caller to tell Marty that he wanted him to leave the suspect's residence. Marty spoke to the caller and told him that he would stay inside until the warrant was served.

The covering team approached the residence and the suspect began shooting. The suspect shot Marty four times. The last shot was the fatal shot. It was a contact wound to the chest of Marty. The suspect took Marty's gun and began shooting at the approaching officers. The approaching officers were kept at bay by the stairs. They were unable to approach the suspect or Marty. They were unable to climb the stairs without being exposed to gun fire.

The officers began to communicate with the suspect in order to have him give up. The suspect told the officers that he would give up once the police had arrived. It became obvious that the suspect was acting as if the officers outside his door were not, in his eyes, cops. The suspect told the approaching officers that he was going to call the police. After much discussion the suspect agreed that in fact the individuals, by the stairs, were police officers. The suspect gave up. Upon their entry into the apartment Gary found his friend, Marty, dead. He attempted to resuscitate him to no avail.

Let's look at the events that transpired and how they could have been averted then and in future occurrences.

First, there should be an unwritten law which states that the covering teams should not approach and try to place a suspect under arrest while an undercover officer is near that individual or inside the same dwelling with the suspect, especially if the suspect is armed.

Undercover operators should try to meet and negotiate with suspects in neutral locations. In other words, they should meet away from the suspect's residence and locations familiar to him.

Simply because the covering team has an arrest or search warrant in their possession, it does not mean that those warrants have to be served at a specific time. Let's say that we have a warrant and intelligence regarding the suspect shows that the suspect has a fully automatic weapon at his disposal and within his reach at all times inside the house. For the most part, with that knowledge in mind, we should enlist the services of a SWAT team to make entry. Sometimes entities do not utilize a SWAT team and undertake the service of the warrant by themselves even though SWAT was better trained and prepared to handle the task. Another way to handle this scenario would be to wait the suspect out. Why not serve the warrant on him when he leaves the house, detain him and go back to the residence with him in custody. By doing this we could ascertain if there are any other individuals inside the house and if they are armed. We have also taken out the chance of having the suspect shoot at the officers while serving the warrant.

It seems like law enforcement officers have a non-reversible mission to accomplish. Once the warrant is signed, it must be served as soon as possible come hell or high water. I would like to think that we have alternatives to that thinking. Each warrant should be approached differently and the safety of the entry and securing of the premises must dictate when the warrant will be served.

In the case of Marty, the covering team should have never attempted to make entry into the suspect's residence with the undercover operator there. Had I been there and had Marty told the phone caller that he would not come out, I would have had the caller phone Marty back and tell him that we were leaving the area. The warrant would only be served after he exited the apartment. The suspect was not about to go anywhere. Leaving was not a problem, Marty had already left once.

No one can say what transpired inside the apartment and what Marty encountered. It is obvious that Marty was not able to shoot at the suspect once the attack began. If this occurred because of weapon accessibility, or not, we will never know. We will never know if Marty would be alive today if he had told the suspect that he was a cop prior to the suspect having fired the fourth and fatal shot. At no time had Marty identified himself.

As a supervisor and close friend to those that I work with, it is difficult to entertain the thought of having one of my decisions cost one of them their lives. Three 1/8 ounces of heroin or the arrest of a suspect are not worth the life of anyone, especially a fine officer like Marty.

A Rip All the Way

The following case involved a narcotics unit. The undercover officer in this case had made two prior purchases from the suspect. The first buy was for one gram of cocaine, the second buy was for one ounce. The last buy would be for a kilo of cocaine. All of the previous buys were made inside the suspect's residence. When it was time for the third buy, the kilo buy, the deal was set up to go inside the suspect's house.

The kilo would be bought for $29,000. The covering team set up in the area of the suspect's house. A van, which contained the point and the monitoring individual, was set up across the street from the suspect's residence.

The undercover operator arrived and parked his car in the driveway. The undercover operator met with the suspect outside and a short conversation ensued. As the suspect and the undercover operator spoke, the suspect told the undercover operator to open his shirt so that he could check him to see if he was wearing a wire. The undercover operator refused to open his shirt and told the suspect that they had done business in the past, that he was not wearing a wire. The undercover operator did tell the suspect, at that time, that he was carrying a gun for his safety.

From the time of his arrival at the residence the undercover operator told the suspect that he was alone and that the money was in the trunk of the vehicle. The undercover operator would repeat these two things to the suspect many times during the negotiations.

The suspect and the undercover operator went into the suspect's house. While in the house, the suspect utilized a walkie talkie and began to talk to a second suspect. This second suspect was driving in the neighborhood, on a motorcycle, trying to detect surveillance units or police in the area.

The suspect in the motorcycle radioed to the main suspect that he had observed a possible surveillance vehicle. He described the vehicle as a thunderbird. The undercover operator again reiterated the fact that he was alone, that no one had followed him to the house and that he had the money in the car.

At one point, during the conversation between the undercover operator and the suspect in the house, two additional suspects who had been hiding in the bedroom emerged. One of the suspects was armed with a baseball bat and one was armed with a hand gun.

The main suspect searched the undercover operator and detected the wire which he was wearing. The suspects began to beat the undercover operator and it took some time before the covering team was able to make entry into the house and rescue the undercover operator.

During the entry by the covering team the main suspect was able to escape through one of the windows.

Looking back at this case, if you were to apply those rules which have been outlined in this book, the attack on the undercover operator could have been easily averted. The undercover operator went into a location which was controlled by the suspect. That placed the operator at a disadvantage from the beginning. The suspect controlled everything that was to take place inside the residence.

Remember the word PERCEPTION. The undercover operator felt safe because his covering team members were in the area. The suspect, rightfully so, PERCEIVED that the operator was an easy mark for a rip off. The previous small buys took place inside the residence and the operator was alone. The operator had always brought the money with him. This time was no different. The suspect perceived that the only thing between him and $29,000 was one individual. This individual, the operator, was under the control of the suspect.

The gun, carried by the operator, was not a deterrent to the suspect. He knew that he had two additional cohorts in the next room. One armed with a bat and other with a hand gun.

Even after finding the wire, the suspects proceeded to beat the under-cover operator. As the operator was being beaten, he verified that the guy in the thunderbird was his brother in law. He never told the suspects that he was a cop. At best, the suspects could have felt that the operator was an informant. Still the beating continued.

For many reasons, the covering team took quite some time before they finally made entry and rescued the undercover operator. At that point there were three suspects beating on one individual.

Simply stated this incident was easy to avoid. Do not handle buys in a location which is dominated and controlled by the suspect. The word is neutral. Use a neutral location. Money management and PERCEPTION are very important. If the undercover operator handles the money like an easy mark he will be treated as such. All that the suspect needs is to PERCEIVE that he can rip off the operator. Once that PERCEPTION takes place in the suspect's mind the rest is easy to predict.

The undercover operator continued to play his undercover role to the end. I have no doubt that during the game planning stages of this case no one ever discussed the fact that the undercover officer should identified himself, as a police officer, when in trouble. Money management was a distant concern. The operator should have never taken the money by himself into the suspect's residence. At that point all of the control and safety, of that money, was lost.

Accidental Shooting

The following case involves an operation which utilized two under-cover operators. One a female the other a male. The operators were dealing with two suspects. One of the suspects was 17 years old.

The undercover operators were negotiating to buy 2 kilos of cocaine for $30,000. The male operator was conducting the negotiations with the suspects.

The male undercover officer did not have a good feeling about the case but he went through with it.

The meet for the buy took place in a large parking lot. The under-cover operators were using a two door, seized vehicle with tinted windows. This meet took place at night and it was cold. This caused condensation to form inside of the windows of the undercover vehicle. This condensa-tion and the window tinting, made it difficult for the covering units to be able to see inside the car.

The plan formulated called for the male operator to meet with the suspects, on foot, in the parking lot. The male operator would flash the money to the suspects and would wait for the arrival of the dope. The female operator would be inside the vehicle.

During the briefing and game planning the sergeant advised both operators that he did not want to have the suspects go inside the operator's vehicle.

Another point which was covered in the briefing was that the operators would always sit in the front seat of the undercover vehicle.

Once the covering team was set up, in the parking lot, the plan was put into place. The male undercover operator met both suspects. The male operator showed the suspects the money. After the money flash took place, the male operator who was wearing a wire took the money to the undercover vehicle and gave the money to the female operator. Rather than drive away, the female operator kept the money and remained inside the car in the same location where she had been all along.

Both suspects were aware of the money and the location where the money was. After the flash they walked away to a parked vehicle. They were supposed to go to a parked vehicle and get the two kilos of cocaine. While at that vehicle, the adult suspect armed himself with a Tech-9 auto which he placed in his waist band. The juvenile suspect was not armed. Both suspects returned to the place where the male operator was standing. After a short conversation the male operator and both suspects headed for the parked undercover vehicle. At this point the flash had taken place and the male operator had not seen any dope. The male operator and the two suspects entered the undercover vehicle.

As the male operator and the suspects entered the undercover vehicle, an unknown covering officer called over the radio that the two undercover officers were seated in the front seat with both suspects sitting in the rear seat.

The covering team could not see into the undercover vehicle because of the combination of the condensation and the tinting of the windows.

As soon as everyone settled inside the undercover vehicle the adult suspect, who was seated in front, pulled out the Tech-9 auto and pointed it at the female operator's head.

The male operator was heard over the wire to tell the suspect a prearranged signal which alerted the covering team to the fact that a rip off was taking place and that the suspects were armed.

Both operators began to fight the suspect who was armed. The male operator was able to take out his gun and shot the suspect. The suspect was killed and the threat was terminated.

As the altercation was taking place, inside the undercover vehicle, the covering team began to converge in order to rescue the officers and arrest the suspects. As the covering team approached they observed a muzzle flash going from the rear to the front of the vehicle.

The covering team members had information which stated that the officers were in the front seat and the suspects were in the back seat. The muzzle flash showed the shot going from the back seat towards the front seat.

The covering team arrived at the undercover vehicle and they began shooting at the back seat of the car in an attempt to neutralize the suspects. In so doing, the covering team killed the male undercover officer and the second suspect. This shooting was not necessary. Both undercover operators had the situation under control. The covering team conducted themselves in a way in which to stop the threat. They perceived that the suspects had shot at the officers.

The female operator was pulled out of the car to safety.

This case, as the other we have read, could have been concluded without harm coming to the operators.

The money flash was handled poorly. The money remained within the reach of the suspects. They PERCEIVED that there was only a male and a female in the way of them and $30,000. The suspects knew they were well armed and taking the money would be easy.

Had the money been removed after the flash, the suspects would have been left with no alternative other than attempt to kidnap the male operator on foot. Had this happened the covering team would have had a better chance to address the situation. As it happened, the covering team could not see inside the undercover vehicle due to the weather conditions and the tinting.

During the planning stages the sergeant had stated that he did not want the suspects in the undercover vehicle. The female operator could have driven away as the suspects began walking towards the car. The male operator could have requested to see the cocaine before entering the car. Neither happened and the suspect took control of the situation.

When the suspects entered the car the supervisor was confronted with a serious decision. Even if he had wanted to terminate the case at that point he was unable to do so. The suspects began their attack immediately after entering the car.

Had the operators followed the sergeant's directions or had the plan called for better money management, this incident would have been avoided.

Once the situation, inside the vehicle, deteriorated to the point that it did it was impossible for the covering team to intercede in behalf of the undercover operators.

This time was the survival time that we have spoken about. As it happened, the operators were able to control this situation on their own. The problem was that the covering team had bad information as to the location of the occupants inside the car and could not see into the vehicle.

Another factor to address is weapon accessibility. The female operator was not able to get to her weapon and use it during the altercation. This could have been caused because of the poor accessibility of that weapon.

This case was a rip off from the beginning. The suspects did not have access to the two kilos of coke. They had planned to rip off the operators.

It is impossible to sit back and say for sure what steps could have been taken in order to avoid this incident from taking place once both suspects were inside the vehicle. I do know that many factors come into play when planning undercover operations. Experience, planning, briefing and execution are most important. We can not allow ourselves to become involved in mediocrity when dealing in high risk operations such as undercover investigations.

Suspects or Police

In Southern California we are encountering several groups of suspects who are identifying themselves as police officers in order to rob or rip off dope dealers. I will cover two cases where the suspects identified themselves as police officers. One attempting to rip off an undercover officer, the other attempting to rip off a dope dealers.

An undercover officer was assigned to pick up an amount of currency that suspects wanted to launder. This undercover officer had done these types of money pick ups on numerous occasions. Every time the undercover officer picked up money there were never any problems. On this case the undercover officer decided to go to the pick up by himself without a covering team. He was aware that nothing had occurred in the past and felt that nothing would happen again.

Prior to leaving for the pick up, the undercover officer spoke to one of his partners and advised him he would be going to make the pick up by himself. His partner was not very busy. He told the operator that he would accompany him as a back up officer.

The officers left and went to the location where the pick was to take place. As with previous pick ups the operator thought that the suspect would arrive, give him the money and leave. COMPLACENCY took over. The operator planned the pick up on this case based on the results of the previous cases. He made up his mind that this pick up would go as all of the others.

Upon arriving at the location the undercover operator met with the suspect. The suspect gave the operator the money bag. After a short conversation the suspect left the area.

As the undercover officer began to leave the area, with the bag of money, three suspects approached. The suspects identified themselves as police officers and placed the undercover operator under arrest.

The partner felt that something was wrong. The suspects did not conduct themselves as police officers. The partner approached and an officer involved shooting took place.

Eventually the suspects were placed under arrest, without harm coming to the undercover officer or his covering partner.

This case could have been disastrous to the undercover officer and his covering partner. Had the operator showed up to pick up the money by himself, he would have been robbed or at the worst he could have been killed.

It is my belief that we will see more rips during money pick ups. Money pick ups are no different than any other undercover operation. These operations have to be handle carefully and with a lot of planning. Any operation, regardless of how simple it seems, has to be approached as if a rip off is about to occur. If we approach these investigations with that in mind, we will be able to handle any changes as they happen.

We cannot base the planning of an operation on previously handled incidents. The planning should be conducted with the worse scenario in mind. The complacency factor cannot be part of the equation.

The next case is a very recent operation. An informant introduced me to a suspect, over the phone, who had a team of suspects who were involved in ripping off dope dealers. I began to negotiate with the suspect. As the conversations continued, the suspect told me that his rip off team was very experienced. They had been involved in ripping off dope dealers for some time. The suspect told me that when this group conducted a rip off, the people being ripped would not be able to tell the difference between the rip off suspects and the real police.

The suspect and I continued to negotiate. We located a house and planned to set up 42 kilos of cocaine in it. Along with the cocaine we would place a money counter, some pay/owe sheets and other paperwork which showed that a cocaine transaction was to take place.

Throughout the negotiations the suspect was very careful about his conversations over the phone. I was able to avoid meeting him in person, conducting all of the negotiations over the phone.

I contacted the suspect and told him that I was in San Diego and that the dope would be in the house the following Monday. I told him that I would not know where the house was located until the morning of the rip off. The suspect wanted more notice than that in order to case the location, but I advised him that it would be impossible for me to find the address out until the day that the rip off was to take place.

On the day of the rip off, we set up the cocaine in the house. A squad took over the surveillance in front and rear of the residence and the security of the cocaine.

After the cocaine and the surveillance were in place, I contacted the suspect and gave him the address and the description of the house.

Within an hour the suspect drove by the house and he checked the location. He continued to check the area. The suspect then left and was seen meeting with a number of individuals inside a van.

Approximately 1 and $1/2$ hours after the first call took place, the surveillance units in front of the house saw a grey van arrive. The van contained four suspects. The van parked in front of the house and a male exited. The male was dressed in a mailman's uniform. The suspect dressed as a mailman took a U.S. POSTAL overnight package and went to the front door of the house. The suspect knocked on the front door and waited. He received no reply. He returned to the van and spoke to the other three suspects. At this point the other three suspects exited the van. The suspects were armed. While the suspect in the mail uniform knocked on the front door, the other three suspects made entry into the house through a rear door.

The suspects opened the front door of the house and they let the suspect, dressed as a mailman, into the residence.

Once inside the suspects fired one round inside the house (It is not known why the round was fired. The house was empty). The suspects took the cocaine and the money counter, exiting the residence.

The suspects entered the van and began to drive away. The units in the front of the house converged on the suspects' van and an officer involved shooting took place.

One of the suspects was wounded. The other three suspects were taken into custody without problems.

At the time of the suspects' arrest, detectives recovered four handguns, a hand-held radio, four sets of handcuffs, three badges which resembled law enforcement badges and a dress jacket from the Los Angeles Sheriffs Department.

We also arrested four other suspects who had been involved in the conspiracy but were not present at the house during the rip off.

During the debriefing of the suspects, we ascertained that they had been involved in prior rip offs. The suspects who went into the house were advised that if they encountered any individuals inside they were to handcuff all of them and put them down on the floor.

These suspects were ready to take any action necessary in order to do the rip off.

We have to keep these types of suspects in mind. Any undercover operator could be approached by a group like this during any undercover case. If that happens and that scenario has not been discussed during the game planning stages, the supervisor in charge of the operation will encounter tremendous difficulty in dealing with the problem.

Unarmed Operator

The following case took place some time ago. The case took place in Dade County, Florida. At the time the leading agency did not believe in having their undercover operators armed. As a matter of fact even the agents who were to cover the operator would only be allowed to carry a revolver.

As a result of this case, the agency changed its policy.

Before we get into the case let me describe the operator and the suspect.

The operator was a male 6-2, 240 lbs in extremely good shape. He worked out and at the time that this incident took place he could bench press in the neighborhood of 300 lbs.

The suspect was a male 5–8, 155 lbs, 40 years old. Harvard graduate, C.P.A., marshall arts enthusiast with no criminal background.

The operator met the suspect at his office. The office was in a commercial area. The windows had wrought iron reinforcement around them. The front door to the office was reinforced with metal and could only be opened from within, with either a key or a button which was, unknown to the operator, located under the suspect's desk.

The undercover operator was at the suspect's office in order to assist him with the laundering of money.

While the undercover operator was inside the office, his covering team was outside, sitting in a car, monitoring the wire. The wire did not work properly so the covering/monitoring team moved closer to the office so that they could pick up the conversation between the suspect and the operator.

After having been inside the suspect's office for some time, the suspect got a phone call from an employee. The employee told the suspect that there was a car, with the windows tinted and antennas, which had been outside the office for a long time. The caller told the suspect that there were two people inside the car and that they had the engine running while they sat outside the office. (Remember this was Dade County and the weather can get quite warm and humid, obviously the covering team had their air conditioner on).

After the phone conversation the suspect got up and went outside to check the vehicle. By the time that the suspect went outside, the vehicle had left. (It is possible that the covering/monitoring team heard the conversation over the wire and left in order to not be seen by the suspect.)

The suspect returned to the office and began to question the operator to ascertain if he thought that someone could be following him. The suspect reiterated that he was clean and that no one would be looking at him. The operator, likewise, told the suspect that he was not being followed. The operator told the suspect that he had a friend who was a police officer who could run the license of the vehicle which had been seen outside. He would find out who they were. The suspect gave the operator the license number of the car.

At that time the operator felt that it would be smart to make an exit, telling the suspect that he was a little concerned about the car outside the office. The operator told the suspect that he would make sure that he was not followed once he left the office. He asked the suspect to check, once he left, in order to ascertain if there was a car that left at the same time that he did.

It was time for the operator to leave and the suspect made out a payroll check, in order to pay the operator for his services.

The operator got up and began to walk towards the front door. As the operator walked away, the suspect asked him if he had served time in the military. The operator replied that he had been in the service but that his job had been of a clerical nature.

Once he reached the front door, the operator turned around and asked the suspect to let him out of the office. The suspect began to walk towards the front door. Without warning, the suspect ran up to the operator and began to strike him. The operator could not understand why the suspect was hitting him. Unknown to the operator, the suspect had an ice pick in his hand and he was not striking the operator, he was stabbing him repeatedly.

The operator realized he was in trouble and began to yell for help. The suspect would stab the operator numerous times and he would then back off, reassessing his prey.

The suspect continued the stabbing. The suspect told the operator he was sorry as he was stabbing him. The operator was stabbed fourteen times.

The suspect searched the operator and found the wire which he was wearing. The operator told the suspect that the I.R.S. had made him wear the wire. He went on to tell the suspect that the I.R.S. had heard everything that had taken place.

Knowing that his back up team was outside and would be unable to make a quick entry, the undercover operator faked his death. The suspect took the operator and placed him on a chair and tied him. The suspect then took a hammer and beat himself on the back of his head, placed the hammer in the operator's hand and laid down on the ground. The suspect was preparing himself for the eventual entry of the law enforcement people who were outside the office. Upon their entry he would use some type of self-defense explanation for what had occurred.

The agents outside the office were having a difficult time as they attempted to gain entry. They had requested help from the Dade County Sheriff.

The suspect got up and began walking around the office. The agents outside, had one of their secretaries call the suspect's office and ask to speak with the undercover operator. As the suspect was speaking to the secretary the undercover operator yelled that he needed help, by that time he had cut himself free. The suspect told the secretary that the operator had left. She played it off very well, making the suspect believe that she had not heard the operator's call for help. The secretary advised the covering agents what she had heard.

The operator picked up the hammer and threw it through a window. One of the agents was able to reach in with his weapon and began covering the suspect. The operator started to run towards the front door. At that time a Dade County Deputy broke a portion of the front door, covering the suspect with his shotgun. The operator convinced the suspect to throw him the keys and was eventually able to make his exit.

The suspect was arrested without further incident. The operator spent the next two weeks, in life support, in a hospital. He had lost 40% of his blood.

Sometime later the suspect was convicted and is serving 67 years in prison.

In this case the operator was very lucky that he made it alive. Let us look at the things that could have made a tremendous change in the outcome of this case.

Of course the biggest factor in this case is the unarmed operator. Had he been armed he could have repelled the attack. Because of that reason I do not believe that any undercover operator should undertake an operation unarmed. At this time, I do not believe there are any agencies with that type of policy.

The mind set in this case was very poor. There is no doubt that the officers involved felt that the likelihood of danger was minimal. This case illustrates the inability, of the officers involved, in being able to forecast the outcome of any operation. Because of this we have to plan for the worse case scenario on every case.

The agents outside felt that the suspect would not be able to see them as they sat outside the office. However, we have to think not only about the suspect, but about associates that we are not aware of. The covering team in an undercover operation cannot become complacent in covering the operator.

Sometimes we will have to sit in a place without air conditioning or other luxuries. By so doing we can cover the operator safely and undetected.

I believe that the operator made too much of the car seen by the suspect's associates. The operator began to talk to the suspect about his contact in the police department who would eventually give him the information on the license plate of the car. The operator has to distance himself from any law enforcement contact and he can not make a big deal of the car or the occupants. It would be sufficient for the operator to say that he was not being followed.

At no time did the undercover operator identify himself as a law enforcement agent. He told the suspect that he was made to wear the wire. In the eyes of the suspect he was dealing with an informant.

It is my belief that the undercover operator was at a tremendous disadvantage when he entered the office. The suspect could do anything he wanted to do and no one could come into the location to assist the operator. In this case the survival time took a long long time. The undercover operator was on his own and there was nothing he could do. The operator was in the suspect's domain and the suspect controlled the operator. The operator in this case was much bigger in size, than the suspect who he was working. That factor made no difference. The suspect had the element of surprise and the control of the premises. The operator was at a disadvantage.

As I have discussed this case during my oral presentation, I have been asked what I would have done if I were faced with the same set of facts. That is a simple answer. I will not become involved in an operation where I do not control 95 percent or more of what is happening. As to the other 5 percent, I make sure that the suspect does not control it. Simply put, I would have not sent an operator into that office under the circumstances which you have just read.

It would be very hard for all agencies to hold to my rules, as they apply to going inside a location. If an agency or a section decides that their officers should be involved in operations where they are to go into dwellings controlled by the suspects, I recommend that they be very careful and not do it while the deal and or money flash are taking place.

No undercover operator should be exposed to any type of injury. This is true even if he works for an inexperienced supervisor. If the policies of an agency are not conducive to the safety of an operator or an operation, the officers within the agency should give the needed input to their command staff in order to make the necessary changes.

Reverse Rip Off

This case took place in Southern California. This case is a recent case and like the other cases it should not have happened. The undercover operator in this case was a very experienced, hard working officer. He had about four years of experience in the field of narcotics enforcement. He was the case agent and the undercover operator on the case.

The supervisor in this case had no prior narcotics experience. He had been working the field of narcotics enforcement for approximately two months prior to this case.

The undercover operator told his informant to put the word out that he knew an individual who had an amount of cocaine for sale. The informant met a couple and they told him that they knew an individual who might be interested in buying some cocaine.

The informant met a suspect through the couple. The informant then introduced the suspect to the undercover operator. The suspect's name was Freddy. On the first meet the undercover operator flashed one kilo of cocaine to the suspect.

The Friday after the first meet, the undercover operator/case agent got a phone call from Freddy. Freddy told the operator that he wanted to introduce him to the main man in the deal. The suspects set the meet to take place at a small strip mall. The officers involved in the operation did not know that the location was very close to the main suspect's house.

On the briefing, prior to the meet, the operator/case agent gave the directions on the case. He told the covering officers that he did not want anyone followed after the meet. The operator did not want to put any heat on the suspects.

The meet was set up and the main suspect showed up with his cousin. They showed up in an older vehicle. When the discussions began, the suspect set up the deal for the purchase of 20 kilos of cocaine. He agreed to pay $20,000 per kilo. The suspect told the operator that he wanted to do the deal on the same day as the meet. The suspect told the operator that he would go and look at the money and once that took place he would get in contact with the operator in order to finalize the deal. The suspects left, not being followed. The operator also left and waited for the call from the suspects.

Within a time span of one hour the operator got two phone calls from the main suspect. On the first call the suspect told the operator that he wanted to buy 100 kilos instead of 20. The operator agreed. On the second call the suspect told the operator that he wanted to buy 200 kilos instead of the 20 or 100 that they had discussed before. The operator agreed. The deal went from 20 kilos to 200 kilos within an hour's time. The price for the cocaine did not drop. The kilos remained at the same price.

While the operator waited for the suspects to call back, he ran the license number of the vehicle which the suspects drove to the meet location. The license number and vehicle had been involved in an investigation by another agency. This information boosted the suspect's background in the eyes of the operator.

The suspects never contacted the operator back on Friday and the case hung up.

On that Saturday the suspect called the operator and wanted to do the deal. The suspect and the operator negotiated back and forth but no agreement was reached. The case was postponed until Monday.

On Monday the suspect called the operator and told him that he wanted to see the 200 kilos. Even though the operator had not seen any money up to that time, he agreed to go through with the dope flash, (had this reverse been successful it would have been the largest reverse ever done in Southern California. The officers would have seized $4,000,000).

The flash was to take place at the same location where the meet took place. The unit in question had, at their disposal, 57 kilos of seized cocaine which they could use for reverse type investigations. The suspect in this case wanted to buy 200 kilos so they took the 57 kilos and made up the difference by placing other articles in boxes which they were to show to the suspects. As of the time of the second meet, none of the suspects had been identified.

The officers placed the boxes containing the 57 kilos and the rest of the make believe cocaine, into the informant's motorhome. A covering team left to cover the motorhome and the informant. The motorhome was placed in a gas station close to the meet location.

The operator drove his van to the meet location. The operator met the suspect and after a short conversation he left to pick up some of the cocaine. The operator went to the gas station where the informant was. They loaded up the boxes, which contained the 57 kilos of cocaine, into the operator's van. The operator drove back to the meet location.

The operator arrived at the meet location and parked. The suspect approached the van. The operator opened the side door of the van and showed the suspect the boxes which contained the 57 kilos of cocaine. After looking at the boxes, without opening them to look inside to see if in fact the boxes contained cocaine, the suspect told the operator that he had to make a phone call. The suspect made the call, returned to the van and told the operator that he wanted to see the complete load, all 200 kilos of cocaine.

The operator left the parking lot and returned to the gas station. Again, the operator had not as yet seen any money. The operator and the informant loaded the rest of the boxes into the van. The operator placed the boxes with the real cocaine towards the front by the door of the van. The boxes with the make believe kilos were placed to the rear. This was done in case the suspect decided to look inside the boxes. The operator asked the informant to accompany him to the location where the suspect was.

The operator drove away with all of the boxes in his van. The informant was seated in the front passenger seat.

While the operator was at the gas station loading the boxes into the van, the surveillance units at the meet location, had seen the suspect making numerous phone calls from a pay phone.

The operator drove back to the location where the suspect was. He parked the van and exited. The suspect approached the van and the operator opened the side door. All of the boxes were exposed to the view of the suspect. The suspect looked inside the van and was surprised to see the informant sitting in the front seat. The informant was a large individual. The suspect backed out without looking into the boxes and told the operator that he was going to go and look at the money. The deal was for the suspect to call the operator back as soon as he saw the money. The suspect told the operator that the deal was to happen inside a house in a white neighborhood. The suspect told the operator that the only people involved in the deal would be he and the operator.

The suspect left and again the surveillance units did not follow him. The suspect called the operator back. The operator was told that the money man was out of pocket. The case hung up.

NOTE: The case had been going on for four days. A 4 million dollars case and the money man was out of pocket. The operator had shown the suspect 200 (what the suspect believed to be 200 kilos of cocaine. Remember PERCEPTION) kilos of cocaine and he had not seen any money. The operator was wearing a wire on this case. All of the conversations between the operator and the suspect were in Spanish. The officer monitoring the wire did not speak Spanish. After each meet the squad was not debriefed well. The only individual who knew everything which was taking place was the case agent and the undercover operator, in this case that was one and the same. The rest of the squad was pretty much in the dark. None of the suspects, these big dope dealers, had beepers. The operator kept in touch with the suspects via a cellular phone.

On Tuesday the suspect called the operator and told him that he was in Victorville looking at some cocaine. The suspect told the operator that after seeing the cocaine in Victorville he liked the operator's merchandise better.

NOTE: Keep in mind that the suspect did not look at any of the cocaine which the operator had, he just looked at the boxes.

On Wednesday the operator did not hear from the suspect. The operator told the informant to go out and try to make contact with the suspect. The informant found Freddy and they were able to locate the main suspect. The suspect told them that he would have the money that night to do the deal. The night passed and the deal hung up.

On Thursday the suspect called the operator, set to meet at a McDonald's parking lot. The meet was to take place at 2 p.m. NOTE: The operator/case agent gave the briefing. He told the crew that if anything went wrong he would shoot his way out of the jam. At the time of the briefing it was unknown where the deal was to go down. The suspects were going to decide the location, how and when the deal would happen.

The operator began to load the boxes, with the 57 kilos of real cocaine and the rest of the make believe cocaine, into his van. At that time the operator felt that the case could be a rip off. Nonetheless the operation continued.

At approximately 2 p.m. the operator, driving his van, arrived at the McDonald's parking lot. The operator met the suspect, his cousin and a third suspect named Luis. After talking to the operator the main suspect and his cousin left and they were followed to a market parking lot near by. The main suspect made some phone calls from a pay phone. The third suspect stayed at the McDonalds parking lot with the operator and the informant.

The suspect and his cousin returned to the McDonald's lot where the operator was. The main suspect told the operator that he wanted the informant to stay with Luis. They were to wait near by until the deal was over. The informant and Luis went to a bar.

The suspect got into the operator's van which contained the dope. The suspect told the operator that he would direct him where to go. They were to go to the house where the money was. The van with the cocaine was to remain in the driveway while the suspect and the operator went into the house. The operator was to count the money at that time. After that the deal would be completed.

NOTE: At this time the operator was still wearing a wire. The monitoring officer did not speak Spanish. The squad did not know where they were going. Their only objective was to follow the van, which was for practical purposes under the direction of the suspect.

The operator drove away with the suspect in the van. The suspect's cousin drove away and followed the van for a short time. The cousin began to drive in a counter surveillance mode for a short time and he then drove up next to the van, gave the main suspect the thumb up and drove away.

The van was being followed by a large squad of officers and a helicopter. The suspect began to direct the operator on which route to take. After driving for some time the operator was told to stop. The suspect got out of the van and began to make phone calls from a pay phone. The operator used the time, that the suspect was in the pay phone, in order to call the officers in the surveillance and bring them up to date. The operator was able to utilize a cellular phone in the van.

The suspect stayed in the pay phone, making calls, for about one half hour. The operator sat in the loaded van during all of this time. The suspect returned to the van and told the operator that he had taken so long because he had to order people out of the house. The suspect told the operator that he did not want anyone present during the deal. The suspects began to direct the operator to a residential neighborhood. The operator was directed to go into a cul de sac and drive to one of the houses at the end of the street.

It was impossible for the surveilling units to drive into the cul de sac. The surveillance and point, of the undercover vehicle and the operator was turned over to the helicopter. The helicopter was flying at a high altitude. The observer, because of the height, did not have a good view of the house and the driveway. The observer did see that the house, in which the operator parked, appeared to be vacant.

The operator parked in the driveway of the house. The suspect got out of the van and ran to the garage in the rear of the house. The garage had been converted into living quarters. A second suspect was waiting by the front door of the garage. The operator walked into the garage. Sometime after the arrival a shooting took place. The operator exchanged shots with the suspects. The operator killed one of the suspects and was shot numerous times in the process. One of the shots severed the bottom of the operator's heart. The operator, who still had two rounds in his revolver, ran out of the garage towards the van. As he ran by the house two suspects began firing at him. The operator shot his last two rounds and fell down on the driveway by the van. He was dead.

The helicopter saw a blue spot on the driveway, the operator was wearing a blue shirt, and as they descended the observer saw suspects running out of the house. The observer requested the surveilling units to enter and contain the area.

The suspects were arrested. The undercover operator was dead. The main suspect was also dead in the garage. In the front house officers found guns and unspent rounds.

A suitcase in the garage, which was supposed to have contained the money, was full of bricks.

This case was a rip off from the beginning.

There were many mistakes made in this operation. Let us look at those mistakes.

The operator met with a suspect who was just a middle man. The operator showed this suspect a kilo of cocaine. The operator was using that cocaine as a prop. In this case the cocaine was flashed very early in the negotiations which was unlike real dope dealers. The first suspect had no business in seeing any dope.

The operator was then introduced to the main suspect. During the briefing, prior to that meet, the operator told the squad not to follow the suspects. The operator was also the case agent. This is unacceptable. The operator cannot be the case agent. He could not make decisions from where he was looking at the case. The undercover officer is not aware of all the things which are taking place. Someone should have stopped this procedure at the beginning of the case. Not to follow the suspects was a mistake. The suspects must be followed in order to identify them and to locate their residences if possible.

From the first meet, from the first few hours, the deal went from 20 to 200 kilos. This was a good indication that something was wrong. This type of increase in the amount of dope, without the price being lowered, is not the way in which real dope deals take place. It usually occurs the opposite way. If the amount that the suspect is going to buy goes up, the price goes down.

The operator placed too much emphasis on the fact that the license number of the car, which the suspects used, was the license number of a car involved in another investigation.

The operator was the individual who kept the deal going. He showed too much interest in the deal. He knew everything, the squad only knew that which he told them.

No doubt the 4 million dollar seizure could have been one of the causes of this mistake. I always remember the saying, it's not the money it's the money. This type of seizure would have been a tremendous accomplishment.

The operator did the dope flash at the request of the suspect, at the location which the suspect chose and in the way that the suspect wanted to do it. It seemed as if the operator would do anything that the suspect wanted and the suspect knew that. The safety of the cocaine was second nature. The deal was placed ahead of the safety of those involved.

At no time did the operator see any money. The case continued even though the money was still suspect. The operator wore a wire and the monitoring officer did not speak Spanish. I have not been able to understand that maneuver. A good monitoring officer can tell if something is going wrong. He is able to do this by the way in which a conversation is taking place. In this case the monitoring officer did not have that ability.

I get very frustrated as I look at this case. This type of case should not have been undertaken past the first meet. Someone should have stopped this case from going forward. If not the supervisor, any of the other members of the squad should have done it.

To place 200 kilos of cocaine (yes there were 200 kilos in the van, the suspect PERCEIVED that, so what the real amount of cocaine was, meant nothing) inside a van and have the suspect direct the operator where to go, is suicide. The suspects PERCEIVED that the only thing between them and 200 kilos of cocaine was the operator. They had a plan to overcome that problem. They felt that the operator was a very inexperienced dope dealer. No dope dealer would conduct himself in the way that the operator did in this case.

The officers in this operation made the rip off very easy for the suspects.

I do know that all of the officers were good officers who were trying to do the right thing. Somewhere the system broke down and it failed. This failure cost the life of a fine young officer and placed a tremendous burden on the rest of the officers, not to mention the family of the officer killed. They will all remember that day for the rest of their lives.

We can not lose sight of our main goal. That goal is the safety and well being of the officers involved in the investigations. I have to reiterate, there is no dope or money worth the life of any officer involved in narcotics enforcement.

While conducting our daily investigations we must ADAPT, IMPROVISE AND OVERCOME while at the same time not compromising the safety of the officers involved.

Chapter 12

PRIVATE INDUSTRY

Narcotics abuse covers all segments of society. Private industry and their employees are not immune.

Within the last few years, private industry has realized the tremendous impact that drug abuse has had in their operations.

Drug abuse, in private industry, can be directly attributed to lost man hours due to illness and on the job injuries. On the job injuries directly impact workers compensation and insurance costs. The productivity and earnings of private enterprise is seriously impacted as a result of employees abusing drugs.

The liability factor for employers, as a result of drug abuse by employees, becomes a hurdle which if not addressed will be impossible to overcome.

Many drug abusers use and sell drugs in their work place. This activity is detrimental to the ability of a private business to be successful. An employee who performs his duties under the influence of drugs, poses a grave problem for his employer and his peers on the job. Individuals working under the influence of drugs become a threat to those around him.

Due to the complexity of the employee drug abuse problem, private enterprise has reached out to local law enforcement in attempts to stop the problem. Many local law enforcement agencies are unable to respond to that call. This is true due to the shortage of funds and manpower which they face.

Because of the need to investigate and stop this type of activity and the inability of local law enforcement to assist, employers have turned to private detective agencies and their own security sections.

Either the private detective agencies or the company security section is directed to place an undercover operative within the work place. This operator's job is to integrate himself into the work force.

Once the operator has been able to become an accepted member of that force, he begins his quest in detecting drug abuse and sales of drugs within the group.

Within the scope of his duties the operator will attempt to purchase narcotics from dealers inside the business. The operator will keep his employer apprised of the different drugs violations and thefts which take place. He will also attempt to build a criminal case against those employees involved in illicit activity.

If the operator is successful in purchasing narcotics, in the workplace, he would have to enlist the assistance of law enforcement personnel.

The operator will be a civilian with no police powers. Depending on the policies of the local law enforcement agency with which the operator and his employers are dealing, the operator will be directed and advised as to how he will handle the purchased narcotics.

Any drugs which are purchased, by the operator, must be booked into evidence at the local law enforcement agency. The drugs have to be analyzed and maintained in order to be used as evidence, in the eventual prosecution of the suspect or suspects in the case.

Due to all of these needs, law enforcement agencies will assign a narcotics officer as a liaison individual in these types of operations. The civilian operator has to contact that officer anytime a drug buy is to take place within the business. The operator and the liaison officer will work out an arrangement for the evidence to be picked up and booked.

If the operation is not restricted to the business and it expands to a location or locations outside, law enforcement personnel must be present during the negotiations and possible drug buys.

The civilian operator is not immune from narcotics laws. He is not allowed to transport, buy, seize or have anything to do with illegal drugs if he is not working under the direction of law enforcement personnel.

It is most important that private enterprise is not sold a bill of goods by unethical private investigation agencies. No civilian involved in private investigations is afforded immunity while transporting narcotics from one location to another.

Peace officers in California receive their immunity under the Health and Safety Code, because of their law enforcement status. The civilian operator is not included under this section.

Undercover operations in private industry are not restricted to incidents involving drug abuse.

Undercover operations can be and are utilized to uncover and restrict employee thefts. Undercover operations are used in the Silicone Valley, in California. The main objects of those operations involve the theft and resale of computer chips and parts.

Chapter 13

LEGALIZATION

The following chapter will address an issue, although not having to do with undercover officer survival, which is very important to me and most officers assigned to the field of narcotics enforcement. This chapter is written to motivate those officers assigned to the field of narcotics enforcement in articulating and presenting the truth regarding drug abuse and putting forth our arguments against legalization of the drugs. We can not remain silent on this subject.

Before I go on I must state that I feel very strongly against the legalization of drugs. I have dedicated most of my career to eradicating the drug problem. I am not looking for job security or any other type of security. I have reached a time in my career when I'm planning my retirement. I listen to many individuals who for different reasons advocate the legalization of drugs.

I have spent all these years in the so called DRUG WAR, and let me say that this is not a conventional war. We are involved in a war like the Vietnam war. A war which, like Vietnam, has been controlled by politicians and special interests. A war which we could have won a long time ago had we received the proper backing and funding.

Many politicians talk the talk but do not walk the walk. They have become more of a liability than an asset in this endeavor.

Let me address some of the myths which we encounter on a daily basis. Myths which are promoted by the press and groups which endorse the legalization of drugs.

It is said that law enforcement is only able to stop 20 percent of the narcotics which come into the country. Well, I do not know how much of the narcotics gets stopped. Why not 30/40/50 percent? How do these individuals arrive at these figures? Do they talk to the importers about the quantity which enters the country? I would like to know what method they use.

As a country we are unable to predict what the deficit will be from one year to the next. Pollsters can't predict who will win an election nor by how much. However, these individuals can tell us that law enforcement can only stop 20 percent of drugs coming into the country.

Another myth is that we have lost the war on drugs. The jails are full and the problem still exists. It is suggested that the best way to handle the problem is to legalize drugs and to tax drugs.

If the jails are full it could mean that we in law enforcement are doing our job by arresting a large number of dope dealers. That others take their place, when they are arrested, is not contested. The real reason that this happens is because our penal system is no longer punitive in nature.

In California prisons prisoners have as many rights as do citizens who are not incarcerated. These criminals are even allowed to have 72 hours of conjugal visits, unsupervised, while serving time. Also in California we have the determinate sentence law. Which means that the prisoners will only serve half of the time which they are sentenced to serve. These people know that if sentenced to 10 years in prison they will serve 5 years and walk away on parole. While in prison they can relax, work out and get three square meals daily, all paid for by the good citizens of the state. This type of sentencing and procedures, while serving time, will only reinforce the fact that crime pays, especially narcotics crimes which yields large amounts of currency to those involved.

Another myth is that by making drugs legal the corruption of law enforcement officers and members of the judiciary will stop.

Law enforcement officers and individuals in the judicial system are no different than any other individuals. Some of them are predisposed to being corrupt. The fact is that a large part of individuals in both fields are not corruptible.

Whether we legalize narcotics or not those individuals who are unethical will continue to be greedy and will continue their quest for money. If not in the field of narcotics, they will appear in other fields confronted by law enforcement. As long as there is money to be had, corruption will exist.

One of the biggest points which is addressed by the legalization movement is that individuals in a free society have the right to make their own choices, even if this means that they will harm themselves in the process. These same people emphasize education and treatment instead of enforcement.

I believe that drug education and treatment are very important. Likewise I feel that enforcement is just as important as the other two.

Society has the right to protect itself from danger. By so doing society will protect itself from what occurs while individuals are under the influence of drugs (i.e., violence to others, theft of property and other related crimes). In today's society drunk drivers and people driving under the influence of drugs kill approximately 50,000 people annually and maim thousands more. Society is making an effort to stop the abuse of drinking and drunk drivers. To legalize drugs at this junction would be equal to sanctioning the killing of innocent people by drivers under the influence of both drugs and alcohol.

The American society has a long record of taking appropriate measures to protect people from their own unwise actions. We have laws which forbid individuals to drive while intoxicated, to deface property, to wear helmets while operating motorcycles and many others.

The actions undertaken by members of society must have consequences. These individuals have to be held responsible for their actions. Society as a whole is not to be blamed for the actions of a few. If we look at the number of individuals who use and abuse drugs frequently we realize that the percentage is very low, (it is estimated that there are 2,000,000 hard core drug users in the country). It would not make any sense to move towards legalization. Legalizing drugs, in order to make its access easier and crime free for two million abusers, would jeopardize the youth in this country. The government would become part of the problem by endorsing such a policy.

Proponents of legalization point out to the fact that despite tremendous efforts made by the enforcement side, prices have fallen while purity and supply have risen. In the fifteen years preceding 1991, I saw drug use and availability rise to the point where the problem, I thought, would become unmanageable. Within the last two to three years I have seen a decrease in the abuse of cocaine and other drugs by the younger members of society. This decrease, I feel, has been brought about by the teaching of drug prevention and the proactive enforcement which has taken place by law enforcement agencies and the rehabilitation movement. Neither one of these alone will be able to eradicate drug abuse. Together they can go a long way to that end.

One of the factors which legalization forces stress, is the price of the drugs. They state that prices have fallen due to the high availability of the drugs. In this market society, in which we operate, a drop in price could also be equated to the fact that there are less users and more dealers which must compete for the trade. This competition causes the price to drop. Maybe there is more cocaine in the market. This could also be true since the number of users has decreased due to all of the efforts in schooling, enforcement and rehabilitation.

The bottom line is that anyone could use figures and charts to represent their cause. Having been in the front line for years, I feel that enforcement is making a difference and is having an impact in the overall problem of drug abuse. Look at the drug seizures, forfeited assets and arrests. All of these factors continue to go up in numbers. I feel that those numbers reflect the tremendous impact which enforcement is having on the illicit trade.

Advocates of legalization argue that by repealing laws which make distribution, purchase, production and consumption of drugs, the number of crimes will be reduced. They further advocate that by giving drugs to addicts, under government supervision, crimes related to drug abuse will stop.

This is an intellectual pipe dream. Our society values must be reinforced and by legalizing drugs those values will be destroyed.

How much drugs will the government supply these addicts? Will they get as much as they want? What about pregnant abusers? Will we become pushers to pregnant women and in the process make the unborn child an addict? If not, these women and others, who we do not supply for whatever reason will have to rely on the black market.

If drugs were legalized and the government does not give these addicts and other users enough drugs to satisfy their addiction, they will turn to the black market. These addicts will become a segment of society with no hope for rehabilitation. There would be no motivation for these individuals to quit their drug abuse.

Legalization forces should look at most of the private Methadone clinics which are in operation. Rather than becoming vehicles to help the heroin addicts in total abstinence in the use of heroin, these clinics have become money making enterprises. The only difference for the addicts is the drug. They have now become dependent on Methadone and most remain with that dependency with no end in sight.

How about the young? Will we legalize drugs to those under 18 years of age? If not, these young people will surely go out to the black market and buy the drugs which they crave. These young people will believe that drug abuse is morally correct. After all, the government would be the biggest pusher in the land. In other words drugs would become morally correct and would be endorsed by our government.

If by keeping these sanctions and spending all of the money we do, in enforcement, schooling and rehabilitation, we can keep one young person from using drugs we have succeeded. For those of you who think that the price, we are paying, is not worth the return think of that young person as your son or daughter. If you do, I am sure you will change your mind.

Legalization is not going to deal with the demand problem that legalization advocates claim exists. Legalization is not the answer. What if we legalized drugs and the experiment failed? What would we, as a society do? Legalization would be a social experiment which would cause tremendous heart aches—an experiment that we, as a society, can not afford.

I have heard all of the arguments which compare drugs to alcohol and tobacco abuse. If we go by that premise we have to go into all of the factors involved.

Rock Cocaine, P.C.P., Heroin and Meth are highly addictive and destructive drugs. To compare them with alcohol is ludicrous. An individual could have a drink and not get drunk. Everyone who uses drugs does so in order to reach a high. Some drinks are tasty. Drugs have no taste as such. The only benefit that an individual would derive from drug use would be his intoxication. With continued use that individual would be addicted.

But looking at alcohol and tobacco, I believe that both are wrong. I use neither nor condone their use. To compare these two substances to drugs, is like saying that by having two substances that are killing our people it is all right to add others. Those new substances would do a better job in our quest to kill or maim our citizens. Besides, whether alcohol and tobacco are dangerous addictive substances, the fact remains that they are legal today.

This so called drug war has not been around for a very long time. Every time that we take a step forward, we find ourselves being knocked back by politicians and budget constraints. If law enforcement was given the proper tools, laws and penal system, the drug problem would be a thing of the past.

We as a society must not allow the media to dictate the proper way in which morality in this country is exercised. Keep this in mind. If drugs were made legal, a high percentage of the minority and poor population would be addicted. This would cause these individuals to become dependent on the rest of society. Legalization would cause an increase in use, much larger than we can imagine.

We as a society can not allow this to happen. The poor and the minority communities must have the same chances and opportunities which all of the other members of our society are afforded. By legalizing drugs we would send a complete generation of disadvantaged youth to their certain death.

Chapter 14

CONCLUSION

This book has covered the dangers which are faced daily by officers involved in undercover operations.

It would be counter productive to state that I have covered all of the answers to the problems which are faced daily by these officers. This book attempts to awaken the reader, causing him to ask himself, and those with whom he works, if they are doing the best job possible in their quest to attain a safe and productive undercover operation.

We, in the narcotics enforcement community, have to deal with court decisions, political pressures, budgets restraints and equipment failures.

Daily we encounter skepticism from the citizens whom we serve and wonder if our dedication and professionalism is ever appreciated.

All of these outside forces should not deter narcotics officers and all other law enforcement officers in the battle to eradicate drugs from our society.

In our attempt to eradicate drugs, we cannot lose sight of the fact that the safety of our brother officers is the most important factor which we must address and face daily.

Our mental preparedness and dedication, to those officers with whom we work, should be second nature. I wish that I had been unable to have written the chapter covering the undercover cases that went wrong. I know that every case which I covered involved real people, people like you and me—individuals who gave this job everything that they had. These fine, dedicated officers left behind their loved ones and their partners. Their death had a tremendous impact on the lives of many individuals. We have to believe that their deaths will have an impact in the outcome of this battle which we fight daily. I cannot believe that they died in vain. These officers were heroes. They should be the role models to our youth.

I would like to dream that in the future no other law enforcement officer will die as a result of their involvement in this field. I know that this dream is unrealistic but I hope that this book will help keep some of you alive.

There are questions that we must ask. Procedures that we have to change. We have to continually assess the ability of those with whom we work. Do not be afraid to speak out if you see someone heading for disaster. I have no doubt that any of you will stop any of your peers who is involved in stealing confiscated money or drugs. Our safety is just as or more important. Speak out. Do not condone an unsafe environment to be perpetuated by inexperience.

Narcotics officers work hard and play hard. We become closely related as a result of our work. I spend more time with the officers that I work with than with my wife. We are family and we can not allow a member of our family to perish because of our silence.

Think safety. Do not forget the word PERCEPTION. Do not underestimate a suspect or suspects. These suspects will take as much liberty, with the undercover operator, as we give them.

Dope or money are not props. They are real assets which will cause someone's death if used improperly.

Supervisors are responsible for the safety of the officers under their command. Do not delegate this responsibility. Face the responsibility and do the best job that you can. I would never ask one of my people to do something I would not do myself.

For seventeen years I have been involved in the field of narcotics enforcement. I have found this job to be the best and most challenging job in law enforcement. I have worked and been associated with the finest officers in the land. If I were to do it all over again I would not change anything.

Keep this in mind. Do not compromise your safety or the safety of those with whom you work. ADAPT, IMPROVISE AND OVERCOME.

DATE DUE

AP 21 98		
DE 8 98		
MY 27 99		
MY 2 00		
NO 10 05		
FE 8 07		

DEMCO 38-296